BATTLING THE BARRIERS TO SUCCESS

50 Ways to Keep Your Workplace Improvement Initiative on Target

JOAN P. KLUBNIK

MARLENE ROSCHELLE

IRWIN
Professional Publishing®
Chicago • London • Singapore

We dedicate this book to all our peers and clients who are struggling with the same implementation issues regardless of their organization's particular tool or strategy. We wholeheartedly thank all those who spent time with us to discuss the trials and tribulations of improvement initiatives. Their insights into their successes and failures provided the raw material that we melded into the 50 barriers.

A special thanks to our families and friends who lived with us through the process of writing this book.

**Times Mirror
Higher Education Group**

Library of Congress Cataloging-in-Publication Data

Klubnik, Joan P.
    Battling the barriers to success : 50 ways to keep your workplace improvement
initiative on target / Joan P. Klubnik, Marlene Roschelle.
        p. cm.
    Includes bibliographical references and index.
    ISBN 0-7863-0794-3
    1. Reengineering (Management) 2. Communication in management.
3. Employee motivation. 4. Problem solving. I. Roschelle,
Marlene. II. Title.
HD58.87.K58 1996
658.4'063—dc20   96–494

Printed in the United States of America
1 2 3 4 5 6 7 8 9 0 BP 3 2 1 0 9 8 7 6

PREFACE

FOR WHOM IS THIS BOOK WRITTEN?

This book is for everyone who has participated or is participating in a workplace initiative. It is written for:

- People on the "firing line" who must be prepared to figure out and then work through corporate endeavors.
- Employees who are changing their roles because of the initiative's installation and can benefit from a handbook to help them identify and deal with potential barriers.
- Change agents who are brought into organizations to resolve unsuccessful endeavors.

Making initiatives work is a challenge that faces people at all levels, in all types of organizations—small and large, manufacturing, financial service, government, nonprofit, health care, and so on. All share a need for practical ideas to make their initiatives succeed regardless of the type of workplace improvement—i.e., re-engineering, business process redesign, benchmarking, total quality management, and mass customization. The book is for those who need a quick reference to identify and categorize issues they face and who want a tool for improving workplace initiatives through prevention and trouble shooting.

WHY USE THE BOOK?

Improvement initiatives employing managerial tools may be the catalyst for organizational improvement, but they do not automatically create permanent change. Many organizations "hit the wall" and waste valuable resources as their attempts flounder. Ineffective implementation usually stems from unrecognized problems embedded within the organization or from lack of continuity between the company's environment and the endeavor.

Without identifying and understanding the barriers, organizations are quick to assign fault to a single factor, such as design flaws, poor planning, or lack of executive involvement. Or they quickly jump from one type of initiative to another without examining patterns of problems.

We came to realize that both approaches are shortsighted. Based on our 40-plus years of work and observation, we suggest that organizations have their own "implementation personalities." These are the paths and patterns that organizations consistently follow, regardless of the type of improvement initiative being implemented. Identifying and categorizing the barriers challenging your organization can help you to determine your unit's implementation personality. This information will allow you to focus on preimplementation preventive actions that will minimize the personality flaws most likely to affect your improvement initiatives. It can also help you to more effectively troubleshoot barriers that your current initiative may be experiencing.

This book highlights these personalities and the associated barriers. Just as with human personalities, studying organizational personalities leads to identifying ways to change implementation behavior. The potential fixes to the barriers are based on interventions used in organizations that successfully implemented their initiatives. We hope that readers will use this book to help identify, confront, and remove their own roadblocks to initiative success.

HOW TO USE THIS BOOK

Readers can use this book in a variety of ways depending upon the stage of the initiative's lifecycle:

- Before implementation as a preventative measure.
- During implementation as a preventative measure.
- When things go wrong (before and during implementation) to assist with trouble shooting.
- To ensure that more of the same is done when things are going right
- To jump start their organizations' initiatives.

It provides a pragmatic approach to figuring out: *how* to keep things from going wrong (preventative) and/or *what* went wrong (trouble shooting). Taking positive action to avoid or correct barriers should be the first step to permanently resolve the root cause of initiative problems. The book emphasizes very achievable, easy-to-use strategies and tools that can be introduced throughout the endeavor's lifecycle. It focuses on tangible aspects of barriers and includes numerous matrices and charts.

The book is divided into four categories: Strategic Positioning and Planning; Communication; The Human Factor; and Organizational Issues. The matrix shown in Table 1 identifies all barriers within a category. Each barrier is numbered to simplify referencing within the text. Additional matrices are included in the introduction to each category to highlight the optimal time to focus on the barriers. Each barrier is addressed in the following manner:

- Self-assessment questions—a quick check to determine if this barrier exists within the organization, including the major danger of ignoring the barrier.
- What needs to be done?—a brief description of the barrier and what can be done about it.
- Why? What are the benefits?—a consideration of the costs to the organization and/or initiative if the barrier is allowed to exist.
- How? A recipe for action—ways of overcoming or minimizing the barrier.
- Who? In what manner?—a look at the key players who need to be involved, who they are and the roles they play in the implementation of the initiative.

Some barriers include a real-life example of how one organization dealt successfully or unsuccessfully with a particular barrier. Because a growing number of organizations choose not to be identified by name in publications, we have provided generic descriptors so that the reader has an idea of the type of organization dealing with the barrier while maintaining the organization's anonymity.

The most effective method for using this book is to complete the self-assessment questions that appear before the discussion of each barrier (or spend some time reviewing the Table of Contents, which highlights all the barrier titles). Either of these approaches will identify barriers that need further exploration. The more identified barriers in a category (i.e., those for which you answered "no" to the self-assessment questions), the more likely the initiative will face constraints.

Once you have a better sense of your organization's "implementation personality," the action ideas included with pertinent barriers can stimulate discussion, lead to more research, and uncover ways to deal with specific obstacles.

A NOTE OF CAUTION: It is important to do *enough* investigation into what is causing a barrier and to identify ways of dealing with it in your particular organization. If this isn't done, quick fixes end up being applied—"Band-Aids" that increase the magnitude and complexity of the barrier. Recognize that no barrier is easy to fix.

TABLE 1

Implementation Category with Associated Barriers

STRATEGIC POSITIONING AND
PLANNING
1. No clear understanding of what *strategic* means
2. Insufficient attention to preplanning
3. Lack of a planning architecture to guide the initiative
4. Initiative inhibited by the organization's expansive boundaries
5. Lack of a holistic plan
6. Lack of balance between analysis and action
7. Lack of environmental information included in the initiative design
8. Lack of documented responsibility for initiative actions
9. Lack of clear focus to achieve the initiative
10. Lack of a committed leader—no one is willing to take a stand
11. The organization's lack of readiness for the initiative
12. Managerial tools become redundant
13. Lack of a clear rallying point
14. No marketing strategy to recruit appropriate support

COMMUNICATION
15. The blind leading the blind
16. People lack communication skills
17. Saturation of communication—all talk and no action
18. Inconsistent communication results in mixed messages
19. Not understanding that everyone wants to know: What's in it for me?
20. Inefficiency of not learning the lessons
21. Lack of *open* communication
22. Inability to harness the informal communication channels
23. Not measuring the effectiveness of internal communication
24. The predicament of making mistakes

HUMAN FACTOR
25. Initiative isn't a reality to top management
26. Not developing the initiative's sponsors
27. Not developing initiative cheerleaders
28. Changes midstream in executive leadership
29. Lack of competent, assertive management
30. Forgetting key parties
31. Not minimizing human foibles
32. Relationship of staff competency to initiative success
33. Not embracing middle management
34. Not fostering creative, visionary thinking
35. Not confronting the resistance to the initiative
36. No time for the initiative
37. Avoiding performance management issues

ORGANIZATIONAL ISSUES
38. Inappropriate reliance on the model
39. Lack of understanding of formal organizational systems
40. Informal organizational structures are sabotaging the effort
41. Unofficial norms and procedures impact the success of the initiative
42. Not considering the coordination costs
43. Not making use of hard data
44. Compensation and rewards are not aligned with the initiative
45. Lack of recognition for small achievements
46. Ineffective evaluation methods
47. Not recognizing customer needs
48. Ineffectual performance appraisals
49. Lack of appropriate training methodologies
50. Allowing inefficient meetings

TABLE OF CONTENTS

STRATEGIC POSITIONING AND PLANNING

Providing a Compass

	Preimplementation	During Implementation
Troubleshooting	10. Lack of a committed leader—no one is willing to take a stand. 11. The organization's lack of readiness for the initiative. 13. Lack of a clear rallying point.	5. Lack of a holistic plan. 6. Lack of balance between analysis and action. 8. Lack of documented responsibility for initiative actions.
Preventative Action	1. No clear understanding of what *strategic* means. 2. Insufficient attention to preplanning. 4. Initiative inhibited by the organization's expansive boundaries. 7. Lack of environmental information included in the initiative design. 12. Managerial tools become redundant. 14. No marketing strategy to recruit appropriate support.	3. Lack of a planning architecture to guide the initiative. 9. Lack of clear focus to achieve the initiative.

Strategy must always be the beginning point for an initiative, because successful implementation depends upon it. The barriers examined in this section reflect some of the major obstacles to effective strategic positioning and planning that initiative planners face. Strategic positioning and planning are the compass for any initiative. They are critical to success because they provide the organization with:

- A vehicle to articulate business goals and direction.
- A tool for resource allocation.
- A decision-making framework.

Bringing them to bear on the initiative rests with the ability and willingness of senior managers to take ownership and to apply the necessary energy.

Positioning results in the initiative:

- Having the right support, i.e., the involvement of key people.
- Being visible to the organization at large.
- Being so orchestrated that pieces fall into place at the right time and in order to have the greatest impact.

Planning is the strategy that allows positioning to succeed. The planning process must:

- Be concrete—ensure that everyone in the organization understands the expectations for the initiative.
- Involve "big picture" thinkers who are capable of scoping out the entire initiative.
- Map out a long-term approach—establish the architecture to guide all phases of the initiative.

> A key is to think broadly enough in terms of the impact of the proposed initiative and look far enough into the future to proactively plan for obstacles that will arise six months or a year into the process.

No Clear Understanding of What *Strategic* Means

	Preimplementation	During Implementation
Troubleshooting		
Preventative Action	✓	

Self-Assessment Questions

1. Has your implementation team agreed upon the meaning of "strategy"?
2. Are you clear on your organization's long-term direction, and is it interwoven into the corporate strategy? Is it accounted for in the initiative's strategy?
3. Before beginning an initiative, is it standard operating procedure to realistically assess all initiative components?
4. Does everyone look to the CEO for strategic direction setting for any endeavor?
5. Is the CEO considered to be a strategic thinker?

If You Answered No, Beware! The organization will be dealing with the initiative at a tactical level only; it will not be taking advantage of the long-range, dramatic opportunities that could be leveraged.

3

WHAT NEEDS TO BE DONE?

A key to understanding strategy is to remember that its primary dictionary definition relates to war—to winning or losing the battle. When applied to a business environment, it connotes that strategic thinkers will define the purpose of the organization and use it as a guide to marshal resources to achieve long-term outcomes.

Senior decision makers own the strategic process associated with any initiative. To manage the process effectively, they must be able to:

- Specifically describe the type of company they want.
- Determine the characteristics that the company should possess.
- Evaluate decisions to ensure that they move the organization in a new direction.
- Assess their bench strength, i.e., the advantages their employees bring.
- Use the strategy to drive the initiative forward.
- Have a very clear picture of what the final outcome should look like and be able to share their view with others throughout the organization.

Leaders need to formulate the organization's reason for being in a stated vision and use the initiative to help it get there. Strategizing will identify the talents and advantage points that can lead to organizational growth and profitability.

WHY? WHAT ARE THE BENEFITS?

The organization must be managed for profitable growth and long-term viability. A lack of clear strategy and purpose leads companies to commit their worst errors. Failure to define the organization's reason for being is a critical omission that leads to poor performance and inappropriate distribution of resources. Strategy is the lever that the CEO can use to move the organization. It provides the basic direction and guides management's decision making. Some of the benefits of strategic leadership include:

- A clear direction that empowers others.

- Measures that can be developed to evaluate the outcomes of decisions.
- A tool to prioritize organizational objectives and determine the related resource requirements.
- The basis that can challenge past assumptions.
- Opportunities that allow for risk taking and creativity.
- Challenges to the infrastructure that supports the old environment.

Those who leverage strategic thinking look far into the future and create plans that will allow them to win the battle. They know how to marshal resources so that they precede the initiative rather than follow after it. This results in faster, more decisive action that outmaneuvers the competition. Their strategic planning better positions them to anticipate future and/or unmet customer needs.

HOW? A RECIPE FOR ACTION

If the CEO is to demonstrate that strategy drives organizational decision making and planning, he or she must incorporate it into improvement initiatives. Initially, this must be done in an obvious way, so that others can begin to understand the role of strategy and apply strategic thinking to their own arena at the micro level.

The strategic process should be woven into both the design and the implementation/maintenance phases of improvement initiatives. In the design stage, the battle plans for the entire campaign are documented. In the implementation/maintenance phases it ensures that the organization does not stray from the initiative. This latter aspect of strategic planning is often forgotten and is frequently identified as the cause of initiative failure.

Strategy reinforcing actions that might be included during the two phases of any initiative are shown in Tables 1 and 2.

During the implementation/maintenance phase, which conservatively constitutes at least 80% of any initiative's lifecycle, the organization must be prepared to take the necessary action to ensure that strategy continues to influence the initiative. The strategy reinforcing actions for the implementation/maintenance phases need to be enumerated before the initiative is implemented.

TABLE 1

Design Phase Actions

Design Phase—Strategy Reinforcing Actions
- Identify the fundamental purpose of the organization.
- Determine where the organization is headed.
- Define the products and/or services provided to customers.
- Determine potential opportunities to impact the business.
- Compare your organization against your competitors.
- Determine how to close the gaps between where you are and where you want to be.
- Determine the competitive advantage to be gained by closing the gaps.
- Develop appropriate measures of success.
- Create and communicate a vision.
- Link vision and values to initiative.
- Identify critical success factors and assign accountable parties.
- Identify barriers, risks, and areas of weakness and vulnerability and establish plans to conquer them.
- Energize the organization around the initiative.

TABLE 2

Implementation and Maintenance Phase Actions

Implementation and Maintenance Phases—Strategy Reinforcing Actions
- Evaluate if strategy and purpose have been followed or forgotten.
- Conduct ongoing reality checks of the appropriateness of the strategy.
- Determine if there is a need to modify the strategy.
- Continue to position and communicate the initiative as strategic.
- Plan for and measure acceptance by the various stakeholder groups.
- Develop commitment and ownership in the workforce.
- Generate shared activities and commitment among the various stakeholder groups.
- Develop tactical action plans to support the strategy; include development and/or revisions to organizational systems such as policies, procedures, performance management, compensation, rewards, and recognition.
- Nurture a culture to embrace the initiative.
- Modify plans when business plans change.
- Review and evaluate progress—create a feedback or continuous improvement loop.
- Re-energize the organization around the initiative.

The designers can use the actions identified in Tables 1 and 2 as self-assessment questions: How does the organization measure up? Are the suggested actions being addressed by the design team?

WHO? IN WHAT MANNER?

Senior managers are accountable for initiative strategy. They possess the global perspective of the organization that is critical to strategic thinking. It is a fact, however, that not all people at the senior level are capable of such thinking.

Individuals responsible for strategy during the implementation/maintenance phases must have demonstrated big-picture thinking in previous long-term assignments. These strategists need to influence key decision makers throughout the organization and must have the tenacity to drive and sustain the initiative.

One predictor of an individual's potential to be effective at developing strategy is his or her reading and game preferences. Often strategic individuals enjoy activities that require forethought and assessing the future impact of immediate actions or that involve retrospection in order to learn from past lessons.

Insufficient Attention to Preplanning

	Preimplementation	During Implementation
Troubleshooting		
Preventative Action	✓	

Self-Assessment Questions

1. Have key players brainstormed actions that will need to be taken throughout the lifecycle of the initiative in order for it to succeed?
2. Have you honestly spent enough time in the preplanning process? Do you avoid the tendency to want to "move on" which can short-change this part of initiative planning?

If You Answered No, Beware! The output of the initiative will be characterized by expensive rework, underutilized resources, and suboptimal return.

WHAT NEEDS TO BE DONE?

Companies need to invest the time it takes to understand the initiative's potential and make key design choices before any other actions are taken. Preplanning is the process that determines the initiative's critical design elements. It focuses on the big picture, scope, purpose, goals, and outcomes of the initiative. Expectations, actions, and accountable parties need to be carefully discussed in light of the initiative's goals. Even when the initiative's imperative is clear, a successful strategic plan remains essential, to ensure that the benefits, value, urgency, desired results, and assumptions that drive the initiative's early phases have been spelled out. A very effective tool to get at this information is a strategic "to-do" task list, which can ensure that all aspects of the initiative are considered.

WHY? WHAT ARE THE BENEFITS?

Detailed, up-front planning lays the foundation for the initiative architecture. A strong start is essential. The good news is that most groups know that planning is important. The bad news is that, too often, not all the critical stakeholders are included early enough to *think the entire process through* in advance.

The initiative's process flows more smoothly when the organization takes the time to formulate a plan. Some of the benefits include:

- The key players are able to create a common framework from which to address the improvement initiative's architecture.
- Involvement in the preplanning process increases the level of buy-in of the stakeholders.
- The process itself provides an opportunity for the team to think the entire change process through and to begin to ensure that all the "ducks" are aligned.

Inadequate preplanning increases the risk of failure because of unclear focus and direction and inefficient sponsorship throughout the process. Senior management must be clear as to what it is they want to accomplish and how the endeavor is linked to the strategic objectives of the firm. There must be no question about why the organization is launching the endeavor. The benefits to the company should be directly attributed to the initiative. Poor preplanning often results in an organization superimposing the initiative on the existing organizational structure rather than determining if basic structural change is a requisite for success.

HOW? A RECIPE FOR ACTION

The use of a strategic "to-do" task list is an effective preplanning technique. The following tips will improve the thoroughness and usefulness of your list:

- *Allow enough time to develop your task list.* Be sure that you keep your audience "captive" by making this an away-from-the-office session with no distractions to interfere. At minimum this process will take one day.
- *Use an external facilitator.* Select someone who is trained to help the group stay on target and who is knowledgeable about the improvement initiative.
- *Do sufficient brainstorming before permitting the critics in the group to speak.* We generally pay people to find fault, so participants are quick to critique ideas. This can limit the list in terms of innovation and thoroughness.
- *Decide upon a minimum list length.* If you are planning through the implementation phase of your initiative, a 20+ item list would not be unreasonable. (To get a final list of this length, you will need to generate two to three times that number during initial brainstorming.)
- *Compile the list and make people from the planning group accountable for results associated with each item.* In some cases the identified person will be a champion to see that the right people get involved to complete the action. In other cases, the person will actively follow through on the item.

A sample strategic "to-do" task list is shown in Table 1. Notice that some items are quite specific and lead to direct, immediate action while others represent activities that will require further research, discussion by key stakeholders and more detailed planning before action can occur. A guide for mapping out your items is shown in Table 2.

WHO? IN WHAT MANNER?

The preplanning team should represent all groups with a strong vested interest in the success of the improvement initiative. Depending upon the scope and breadth of the endeavor, potential members might include: the most senior person(s) within the business unit, key customers/suppliers, process owners, knowledgeable end users, key players from other areas that are impacted

---

TABLE 1

Sample Strategic "To-Do" Task List

Critical Tasks for a Process Improvement Initiative

- Desired outcomes
- Assess organization's capabilities
- Cultural changes
- Project name
- Vision statement
- Value created
- Strategic goals
- Assumptions
- Create model for a process road map
- Description of characteristics of stages of adoption
- Statement of risk if not initiated
- Barriers to roll out
- Customers served—expectations met
- Support systems required/needed
- Organization structure needed
- Top management's role
- Team management (involvement)

- Communications plan
- Cost benefit/cost avoidance analysis
- Reward and recognition
- Competitive benchmarking
- Coaching/assessment process
- Management behaviors
- Performance management changes
- Business/economic impact or environmental scan
- Resource requirements
- Strategy review
- Roles and responsibilities
- Technology requirements
- Orientation and training approach
- Follow-up training method
- Understand the risks of the initiative
- Evaluate success of roll out and training

TABLE 2

To-Do Task Item—Action Map

Strategic To-Do Task Item	Accountable Person	Project Phase	Action That Will Be Accomplished Next	By When Will Action Occur?	Status, Follow-Up, Notes

directly or indirectly by the initiative, experts on the theory behind the initiative, and people who have communication and marketing expertise.

A NOTE OF CAUTION: Sometimes the initiative sponsors don't look far enough down the process chain to recognize whom to include in the preplanning process. To compensate for this, the facilitator must make sure that the group asks itself these questions:

- Have we included all the critical players?
- Have new names surfaced since we assembled the original group?
- Do we need to go back and look at our list again?

READING 2–1

The spokesperson of a Baldrige Award-winning company identified the use of their strategic development task list as one of the critical factors that led to their successful integration of total quality management (TQM). The process gave them a clear road map of items that needed to be addressed throughout the implementation cycle.

Lack of a Planning Architecture to Guide the Initiative

	Preimplementation	During Implementation
Troubleshooting		
Preventative Action		✔

Self-Assessment Questions

1. Has the vision for the initiative been shared throughout the organization?
2. Does everyone understand the vision; i.e., can they see how it ties into their organizational roles and contributions?
3. Have you developed a strategy to support the implementation of the vision?
4. Do you include people with different knowledge and views in the planning process?

If You Answered No, Beware! The ship is going out to sea without a destination or rudder.

WHAT NEEDS TO BE DONE?

It is imperative to establish an architecture—a written vision, strategy, tactics, and specific actions—for the improvement initiative. Executive management—the final decision makers—own this step because they are in the best position and knowledgeable enough to link the vision and benefits of the initiative to the business goals. They must develop and share the vision, which is supported by strategy, tactics, and specific actions. Combined they help people to understand the value of the initiative and how it fits into the overall corporate strategy. They provide a catalyst for galvanizing the organization into action.

WHY? WHAT ARE THE BENEFITS?

The planning architecture is a roadmap that spells out for the organization what is valued, what is important, where the organization is going, and why it's going there. A well-managed planning process not only creates the target but begins to move the organization toward its vision. Having an all-encompassing planning architecture is the first step.

Clear senior leadership, evidenced by a clear plan, helps people to see the possibilities that can result from implementing the initiative. The plan ensures that a consistent message goes out to the organization.

HOW? A RECIPE FOR ACTION

The goal is a clear architecture that will guide the initiative through the design and implementation/maintenance phases. One technique is to use simple, non-work related analogies, e.g., taking a trip, to help people understand their mission. People are often confused by the nomenclature of planning and get hung up arguing about semantics—i.e., what is a vision, what is strategy? They lose sight of the initiative's planning process.

Relating the architectural plan to everyday events helps people to agree on terminology and focus on content. In the example in Table 1, non-work and work-related scenarios demonstrate how you might use an everyday experience and a business example to help explain what is required at each point in the initiative's

TABLE 1

Building the Initiative's Architecture Through Analogies

	Taking a Trip	Business Example	Our Improvement Initiative
Vision	Describe the destination	We deliver competitive products and services on time to our customers	
Strategy	Select the best mode of transportation	Deploy resources through product groups	
Tactics	Develop detailed plans to acquire and use the selected transportation mode to reach the destination	Invest in technologies, using capital markets to produce earnings that can enhance our position	
Specific Actions	Develop the milestones to guide and measure progress in reaching the destination	Become acknowledged as a leader in industry; benchmark against world-class practices, measure by net earnings/return on investments, customer satisfaction, and customer retention	

architectural plan. The space in Table 1 between strategy and tactics indicates a breaking point—items above the space represent big picture strategy; below the space, execution. The next step is to introduce this model into your improvement initiative.

The planning process is best accomplished in facilitated group sessions. Also, hold a session for the senior team to create the vision.

WHO? IN WHAT MANNER?

At different points in the planning process different groups of people will need to be involved.

Notice in Table 2 that as participation is driven downward through the organization, individuals with more knowledge of day-to-day activities are needed. There is a danger in trying to

TABLE 2

Guide for Selecting an Initiative Planner

Planning Step	Who Needs to Be Included?
Vision	Executive managers—the person or team who has the global perspective and the power to ensure that the vision is implemented.
Strategy	Functional area executives, business unit senior managers and key individual contributors who understand the big picture and the organizational limitations that will impact options that might be selected to implement the vision.
Tactics	Middle managers and key individual contributors who are directly involved in the design of the initiative's implementation plans. These people have a vested interest; they understand and are positioned to influence business decisions. (When not included, they often assume they don't have a vested interest and can sabotage the plan.)
Specific Actions	Individual contributors and team leaders/managers who understand the initiative's value to workgroups are directly responsible for the execution of the tactics. These people best understand what needs to happen to implement the vision at an operational level.

have senior-level people make decisions at a technical level. Just as in building a house, the contribution of the architect is different and occurs at a different point than does that of the framer and/or finish carpenter.

A NOTE OF CAUTION: Thinking skill sets are not necessarily equated with organizational position. Recognize that different skill sets are needed as the planning process becomes more detailed and to then draw those with the required skills into the process.

Initiative Inhibited by the Organization's Expansive Boundaries

	Preimplementation	During Implementation
Troubleshooting		
Preventative Action	✓	

Self-Assessment Questions

1. Can the organization adapt the initiative to address the differing needs presented by a global perspective?
2. Are mechanisms in place to help units deal with cross-continent boundary issues that might impact the organization's ability to implement an initiative?
3. Are the global issues considered challenges and opportunities to make the initiative more robust?

If You Answered No, Beware! Uneven implementation will be the result, based upon the initiative's applicability to/receptivity of each business unit.

WHAT NEEDS TO BE DONE?

Companywide initiatives need to be interwoven into the fabric of the organization when the organization is functioning in a global arena. This requires that the endeavor be integrated throughout all business units. In a widespread, global environment, the Pareto Principle (the 80-20 rule) supports having a generalized architecture that establishes basic requirements and elements for the initiative that all must adopt. A certain amount of customization will augment plans to ensure that the global design fits into the local requirements.

The organization should take advantage of the capabilities of each locale and incorporate generalizable strengths into the design of the global solution. This is achieved through interviewing (and if feasible observing) key stakeholders at each site. The process needs to be carefully orchestrated to avoid favoring operations of one or two sites.

WHY? WHAT ARE THE BENEFITS?

As business boundaries expand, the company needs to adjust to the new rules and expectations and improve the way it operates. Increasing customer expectations (internal as well as external) and expanded international standards (e.g., ISO 9000) are mandating that companies competing in the global arena regularly look at what they do and improve their performance.

Organizations often use initiatives to help review, rethink, and redesign so they can leverage their competitiveness. They must consider the arena in which they currently operate—and others in which they intend to operate—and evaluate performance against the competitive standards.

Initiative designers must recognize that, in a global environment, sites need the flexibility to meet the demands of regional and national business constraints. By having a flexible, generalized initiative structure, businesses can tailor initiatives to global as well as local needs. This is a critical factor driving acceptance of the initiative at all locations.

HOW? A RECIPE FOR ACTION

The most difficult problem with initiatives is making them "fit" across an entire organization. This problem is exacerbated when the organization is international. Table 1 provides basic criteria that should be considered when implementing a global initiative.

Beyond these items, a design team will need to conduct an organizational assessment with key people from each locale to determine features of the initiative that need to be adopted globally. These are the elements that the design team must focus on since uniformity is required. Once the initiative's design is finalized, the key players from each locale need to review and collectively accept the plan. The plan should include an element of customization that allows a site to include additional features that it deems important based on the local needs of the division. Such plans need to be integrated into the master initiative.

TABLE 1

Criteria for Global Implementation

- *Develop Requisites*—Include common features, such as operational and tactical plans, critical success factors, manager accountabilities, measurements, documentation, reward and recognition, etc.
- *Talk the Same Language*—Consistently, collectively apply definitions and concepts across the entire organization. This makes it easier for people to communicate and comprehend.
- *Compare Strategies and Tactics Across Business Units*—Learn from best practices within the organization. Encourage sharing of information across global boundaries to build upon the accumulated, cooperative learning of the entire company.
- *Use International Standards As a Guide*—Assess the organization against accepted standards in the global environment. Determines the company's strength and weaknesses on a global scale.
- *Establish Ownership of the Process*—Select owners from each site. Provide them with the authority and accountability to manage the process. They need the passion and devotion as well as knowledge and skill to make the initiative a reality.
- *Assimilate Initiative As a Core Value of the Organization*—Ensure that the endeavor is not seen as a program which has a beginning and end. It is an ongoing requirement for management performance.
- *Allowance for Customization*—Recognize and accommodate the diversity issues that require flexibility and are driven by the initiative's being implemented at a global level.

WHO? IN WHAT MANNER?

The initiative design team comprises representatives from each of the different locations. Those selected for the team must understand the needs of their locale and the needs of the global organization, while being sensitive to differences present in other locations. Some of the skills that will be required in team members include:

- A high level of understanding of diversity issues.
- A big picture view of the organization.
- Awareness of the competitive environment and its potential effects on the company.
- Clear understanding of customer needs and expectations.
- Business acumen.
- Awareness of various international standards and criteria.

It is not expected that each team member will possess every desired skill. The senior managers must make sure that the design team as a composite possesses all the requisite skills.

READING 4-1

When a manufacturing company was implementing an integrated, global software package, it designed the applications to satisfy 85% of the requirements of each site. This resulted in all sites accepting the design because their basic needs were met and each site had a 15% window of customization.

Lack of a Holistic Plan

	Preimplementation	During Implementation
Troubleshooting		✔
Preventative Action		

Self-Assessment Questions

1. Are some of the same people involved with the initiative today as were involved in its design phase?
2. Do people talk about "the initiative" rather than about discrete parts, creating a sense of different owners and participants?
3. Are people as excited about the initiative today as they were during its design phase?

If You Answered No, Beware! Fragmentation of planning and execution leads to loss of engagement, momentum, and results.

WHAT NEEDS TO BE DONE?

Implementing an improvement initiative must be considered as a continuum. Individuals cannot be allowed to think of the initiative as several discrete processes that are grouped together—i.e., design/implementation/maintenance, conceptual/action, identify/select/design/execute—and owned/sponsored by different individuals. The initiative needs to be viewed from a broader perspective that doesn't allow it to be divided up into independent activities.

WHY? WHAT ARE THE BENEFITS?

Too many shifts of responsibility between the stages of implementation have a negative impact on adoption. Such hand-offs slow down the process and reduce the power of the initiative. Typical process issues that must be addressed every time the implementation team membership changes include: reeducation, reorientation, rebuilding team relationships, reviewing history and data, and establishing credibility within the group.

Several different phenomena can occur when the baton is inappropriately passed between phases of an initiative.

- In one scenario, a lower-level person is sanctioned with each successive wave of involvement. The organization recruits the best people for the initiative at first; but by subsequently involving new people in successive stages, it subtly makes the statement that the "new initiative phase" is less important, because people who have less clout in the organization are enlisted.

- In the reverse scenario, the people who are asked to make recommendations for the initial implementation team are not committed themselves, so they do not suggest the best candidates. As the initiative gains credibility, senior managers realize they should have included better people from the outset. As the caliber of participant improves, the initiative experiences a metamorphosis. This may necessitate redoing much of the initial work and delays the process.

Approaching the initiative holistically prevents barriers from surfacing between stages. Typical hurdles that can result from segmenting the initiative are:

- We/they attitudes—"our team versus your team."
- A decline in the level of commitment based on people valuing the initiative less or less dynamic tasks being assigned to successive groups.

Both of these barriers interfere with achieving the goal of the initiative. They drain energy and direct it away from achieving outcomes.

HOW? A RECIPE FOR ACTION

Initiative designers must plan for ways to link the stages of the initiative to the skills required at each phase. This brings continuity to the implementation process.

Team members are only selected and changed if they fulfill pre-identified criteria that support the endeavor. One technique is to focus first on the people requirements of the initiative and then select participants based on their ability to satisfy these requirements.

> An initiative is like an onion. It must first be regarded as a whole, then peeled and each layer thoroughly dealt with.

"What skills are needed?" should be a question that is repeatedly asked by the design team.

Focus on *what is* to be included, not on *who* the individual is. Potential points that must be considered in selecting implementation team members are shown in Table 1.

Once the criteria for inclusion have been developed, several candidates can be identified for each phase. If any rotation is to be done, it will be important to do it gradually. A staged rotation allows for easier assimilation of new members and maintains the continuity of the group and the holistic nature of the initiative. At the end of the rotation, visible awards should be given for participation, and placement in an equal or better position is suggested.

TABLE 1

Bases for Team Participant Selection

Considerations	Criteria for Inclusion—Organizational Role and Skills Required by Phase					
	Design Phase— Accounts for Approximately 10%* of Total Lifecycle of the Initiative		Implementation Phase— Accounts for Approximately 20%* of the Total Lifecycle of the Initiative		Maintenance Phase— Accounts for Approximately 70%* of the Total Lifecycle of the Initiative	
Critical events during the phase—what skills are needed?	Critical event	Skills	Critical event	Skills	Critical event	Skills
Organizational contacts that the individual should bring/have.						
Type of power needed during the phase (e.g., positional, knowledge, association).						
Nature of message that needs to be shared during the phase by the individual.						
Technical competencies needed.						

*These are average time frames. You will need to adjust them for your particular organization.

WHO? IN WHAT MANNER?

Those initially selected for the implementation team should be key people from each business unit who have a vested interest in the initiative and the clout to influence others. Everyone needs to understand the importance of a holistic approach to the initiative, which implies some degree of participation throughout the life of the endeavor. Some traits to consider:

- Belief in the initiative.
- Endurance.
- Corporate visibility and credibility.
- Initiating and follow-through skills.
- Organizational skills.
- Influencing relationship building skills inside and outside present domain (sphere of influence).

Selection may be done by the senior sponsors/managers of the initiative, or this person(s) may delegate an individual or team to identify and possibly appoint potential candidates.

Lack of Balance Between Analysis and Action

	Preimplementation	During Implementation
Troubleshooting		✓
Preventative Action		

Self-Assessment Questions

1. Do the initiative teams have a clear picture of the timeline and expectations for the initiative?
2. Is each group member aware of his or her preference for analysis or action? Do other group members agree with these self-assessments?
3. Can the group describe the general flow of the initiative in terms of accomplishments?

If You Answered No, Beware! Imbalance results in poor implementation—either no signs of achievement, benefit, or results, or too much "shooting from the hip."

WHAT NEEDS TO BE DONE?

The scale in Figure 1 reflects the balancing that characterizes successful improvement initiatives. Organizations at the extremes are characterized by imbalance. The scale will be tipped to one end or the other.

Organizations that are most effective have considered the implications of allowing the scale to tip in either direction. They seek the point at which adequate analysis of the situation and detailed strategic and tactical planning are complemented and balanced with timely action.

WHY? WHAT ARE THE BENEFITS?

Gaining balance prevents problems that occur when too much attention is paid to either analysis or action, as shown in Table 1.

HOW? A RECIPE FOR ACTION

To create a systematic approach, the organization must define balance as it applies to the particular initiative. Factors that need to be considered when defining balance are shown in Table 2.

The items in this checklist represent the minimum. These factors must be assessed by the initiative team to establish balance. The initiative's sponsor should provide a reality check of the group's self-assessment and gather feedback by sampling employees, outside peers, and customers to determine if the group is maintaining appropriate balance. Once agreement is reached, action plans will need to be initiated.

FIGURE 6–1

Organizational Action Balance

TABLE 1

Dangers of Imbalance

Too Much Analysis	Too Quick to Action
▪ People lose interest—they have no knowledge or forget that an initiative is even being worked on.	▪ People haven't been prepared for the change—inadequate communication, education, and planning to prepare them for the initiative.
▪ Loss of timeliness—the window of opportunity for the initiative to satisfy a need has passed.	▪ Chaos and loss of control—things are happening too quickly, no boundaries have been set, people fear change.
▪ People become fearful because they have too much time to dwell on changes.	▪ People fear change because they don't know what to expect.
▪ People are lost in data and facts—overwhelmed with the amount of information presented to support the initiative, they cease paying attention.	▪ No one has any answers or is prepared for the "expected" questions and problems that always surface with any improvement initiative.
▪ Developers and supporters lose credibility because nothing is happening.	▪ Developers and supporters lose credibility because there is no evidence of action, no alignment of support systems, and no recognition of accomplishments.

WHO? IN WHAT MANNER?

Senior managers and division heads must gain consensus on the definition of balance and see that balance is maintained by initiative teams. This will occur if they are clear on their expectations for the people involved in the initiative. They must also provide ongoing feedback and direction to those directly managing the initiative so that rebalancing can occur if necessary.

READING 6-1

An engineering group, true to its analytical style, believed that everything produced by the group had to be absolutely perfect. When it was charged with redesigning itself, the process ended up taking too long, with too much detailed information produced. Because only perfect design was acceptable, no one was kept in the information loop during the process to either provide information or evaluate progress. When the new design was introduced, it was not well received, and the rest of the company gave the new organization limited support.

TABLE 2

Checklist of Minimum Requirements for a Balanced Initiative

Addressed in Our Initiative		Critical Requirements
Yes	**No**	
		Has an assessment of earlier initiatives been completed to determine whether there is a pattern of either hasty implementation or procrastination?
		Has a clear timeline for the initiative been established that includes milestones for specific phases? (See Barrier 9: Lack of clear focus to achieve the initiative.)
		Will the timeline create a perception of inconsequential action taken too late?
		Is there a balance of people-processing styles on the project that ensures an equalization of analysis with results? To achieve this, the team will need: ■ Resourceful people who are good at seeking information to support an initiative and can deal with sudden direction changes based on new information. ■ People who keep track of deadlines and push the group toward meeting them.
		Have macro-level implementation plans been shared and collectively agreed to? Does everyone understand the initiative's deliverables?
		Is a sponsor positioned outside the initiative team who can assess progress and demand more analysis if actions lack substance and push for outcomes if timelines are not being met?
		Have goals, assignments, and performance expectations been established for the team, along with rewards and recognition?
		Are feedback mechanisms, from within and without the team, in place to constantly monitor balance and make adjustments as required?

Lack of Environmental[1] Information Included in the Initiative Design

	Preimplementation	During Implementation
Troubleshooting		
Preventative Action	✓	

Self-Assessment Questions

1. Does the organization understand the importance of environmental reviews?
2. Does the organization use a balance of internal and external data?
3. Is the organization conducting frequent, broad-based reviews to stay competitive?

If You Answered No, Beware! The organization will be incapable of scanning the horizon for future business opportunities and growth.

---

1. Environmental reviews/scans look at economic and competitive trends outside the organization for comparison. Included are variables such as political, technological, demographics, and other trends.

WHAT NEEDS TO BE DONE?

An initiative must be indicative of future trends and be resilient enough to deal with the unexpected and the unknown. Its designers need to look beyond typical forecasts of organizational and economic shifts and estimate indirect and unanticipated changes. What emerges is a more realistic account of the future environment which should influence decision making.

The organization also needs to evaluate internal trends and compare them to what is needed to reach a richly envisioned future state. It should look at historical, operational, and financial data and consider how the organization achieved these outcomes. Anomalies in these factors should influence initiative design. They can accelerate the implementation or modify a stage of the plan so that the endeavor is more reflective of the changing conditions.

WHY? WHAT ARE THE BENEFITS?

Omitting the environmental review can inhibit execution. The comparison provides information about possible future impacts and trends and potential obstacles; furthermore, it highlights areas of the business that have been ignored. The information is gathered and analyzed by the implementation team, incorporated into the architecture, and used to choose appropriate goals. Managing the information increases the endeavor's probability of success.

HOW? A RECIPE FOR ACTION

It is important to assess the internal and external business conditions of the organization. The team should begin by creating a diagram of the current and future trends that may affect the organization. Some common attributes are listed in Table 1. The team needs to verify audiences—present and potential customers, suppliers, and competitors. Rapidly changing market conditions are causing many industries to alter the arenas in which they do business.

The next step is to gather and synthesize competitive and financial data that already exist. Start by determining what additional information to assemble and then discuss methods for collecting the data. The organization can gather the information to expedite the search by relying on internal resources or engaging a third party research firm. Some companies use outside research firms to ensure that the inside perspective does not taint or bias information gathering. Others prefer that their own people gain the intimate knowledge of the information that results from involvement in data analysis.

Next, the team will need to collect information about trends from key stakeholders, using such common methods as questionnaires, interviews, or focus groups. Sampling techniques will dictate the number of people to include. Although there are benefits to involving a large sample, the time constraints that this approach poses must be weighed. A focus group helps to alleviate the time issue but requires skilled facilitators.

After arranging and comparing the information using a table such as the one shown as Table 1, the team will need to:

- Identify issues and obstacles that may prevent successful implementation.
- Identify methods to measure the potential ramification of the issues and obstacles.
- Develop suggestions on ways to overcome the high-impact hurdles.
- Build these ideas into the design to the endeavor.
- Update the data to ensure that the initiative remains on course.

WHO? IN WHAT MANNER?

The senior management team needs to manage the process of environmental review. With their comprehensive perspective, they should identify the trends that need to be studied. Actual review needs to be done by open-minded individuals who can offer an extensive, cross-functional, global perspective to the gathering and assessment of the information.

Due to the time it will take to collect the data, senior management may charter two groups to collect the information—one to address internal conditions and one to look at external factors. The advantage is that two groups minimize the possibility of inaccurate

T A B L E 1

Environmental Review Attributes

| | From the Perspective of* | | | | | |
Current Trends	Employee	Supplier	Regulator	Financial Analyst	Competitor	Customer
Limitations of current business						
New or lost revenue opportunities						
New or lost markets						
Company politics						
Unmet/emerging/unexpected customer needs						
Production inefficiencies						
Unexpected Changes						
Government regulations						
Human resource issues						
Pricing issues						
Distribution channels						
Technology development						
Issues raised by environmental/ consumer groups						
New product development						
New service enhancements						

* It is not expected that you will be able to fill in every column for all trends.

33

and premature assumptions. The team members should be proactive thinkers who can look at information from various points of view. Senior managers need to be open and prepared to use the information gathered by the team to modify the initiative design, based on the team's suggestions.

Lack of Documented Responsibility for Initiative Actions

	Preimplementation	During Implementation
Troubleshooting		✓
Preventative Action		

Self-Assessment Questions

1. Has the organization informed responsible parties of their accountability for specific initiative actions?
2. Do individuals know that they have been appointed to action items?
3. Is there written documentation spelling out responsibilities?

If You Answered No, Beware! Without published accountabilities and involved employees, no progress is made towards accomplishing the stated initiative goals.

WHAT NEEDS TO BE DONE?

Successful initiatives begin with comprehensive and systematic strategic planning. Once planning is finalized, strategic account-abilities must be specifically defined and verified.

A written document outlining the initiative responsibilities should be developed and distributed to:

- Those with responsibility, so they have a clear picture of what is expected of them and others.
- Other key individuals, to ensure follow through on accountabilities and full use of potential resources.

This dual distribution helps to identify potential gaps in account-abilities and highlights opportunities to involve other employees who may be valuable resources but were overlooked. The documentation should be tailored to the specific needs of the organization. Its measure of effectiveness is that it provides a guide and reference that all levels within the organization can access during the course of the initiative's lifecycle.

WHY? WHAT ARE THE BENEFITS?

Implementation can become unwieldy if accountability is not established. Critical time can be lost figuring out who does what if responsibilities are not well-defined.

Documentation ensures that all accountabilities are recorded and that there are no overlaps and gaps. The documentation process highlights the *who* and *what* of any initiative. Putting this information in writing helps the organization to identify dupli-cate efforts or missed areas. It encourages people to take owner-ship because accountabilities are public knowledge. It also identifies those in the company that have not "stepped up to the plate" and those that are too involved. It serves as an accountabil-ity record for performance management, which increases the probability of achieving outcomes and the initiative's mandate being enforced.

HOW? A RECIPE FOR ACTION

The accountabilities can be outlined in a Responsibility Planning Grid. The one shown in Table 1 is a sample of a people-focused model. It might also be appropriate to customize the columns to reflect functional units, geographic locations, and so on.

Selecting the accountabilities for the grid requires holding a meeting with all the key stakeholders to discuss and collectively agree on the items.

A facilitator who is removed from the initiative should conduct the meeting. The role of stakeholders is to:

- Provide input.
- Recommend items to be included.
- Identify areas for which they should take ownership.

The stakeholders must participate openly and honestly in the processes of selection and assignment. This builds trust and helpfulness across work units, which are important conditions for initiative success. If conflict should arise, the facilitator would guide the discussion toward consensus and resolution and minimize "turf issues." The executive manager "owns" (directly or through an appointed representative) the entire responsibility planning process—he or she should have the final authority to make changes to the appointments.

The grid needs to be shared broadly across the organization to ensure that resources and accountabilities are known. Once accountability is finalized, a responsibility cannot be argued. This allows the company to focus its energies on initiative action.

WHO? IN WHAT MANNER?

Stakeholders who are business unit experts and who represent multiple levels and functions within the organization need to be involved in constructing the grid. They must have clout and be able to offer cross-functional views. Some mature organizations may choose to include customers and suppliers in this group.

A facilitator is often needed to drive the responsibility planning process. This person should have an overall perspective of the initiative and be acutely aware of potential areas of accountability.

TABLE 1

Responsibility Planning Grid

Areas of Accountability	CEO	Vice President	Division Head	Manager (List Any Manager Who Is Responsible)	Employee	Workgroup
Who is accountable for sponsoring the initiative—what are the specific accountabilities?						
Who specifically is accountable for promoting the initiative?						
Who specifically is accountable for assuring that the endeavor is timely and is accurately presented to the organization?						
Who specifically is accountable for developing initiative policies, controls, and procedures?						
Who specifically is accountable for developing the critical success factors?						
Who ensures that the initiative "hangs together" and is integrated throughout the organization?						
Do people who are accountable know that they have the above responsibility?						

Furthermore, he or she should be an expert in team dynamics and conflict resolution in order to minimize old organizational and turf boundary issues. This individual will need to ensure that all elements of the initiative's plan have been accounted for in the final document.

Lack of Clear Focus to Achieve the Initiative

	Preimplementation	During Implementation
Troubleshooting		
Preventative Action		✓

Self-Assessment Questions

1. Does your workforce understand and become accountable for achieving the initiative?
2. Do you treat initiatives as interconnected pieces rather than stand-alone processes?
3. Is your initiative linked to the business unit's strategic plan of the company?
4. Is your initiative tied to corporate performance?

If You Answered No, Beware! Workgroups will not contribute, and will become expensive spectators.

WHAT NEEDS TO BE DONE?

Operational business managers need to determine, manage, and deliver the critical success factors (CSFs) of the initiative. When priorities are clear, the workforce knows where to place its energy to attain value-added results. The CSFs guide the initiative because they provide a concise list of what the organization must do well if it is to survive and thrive. They must be linked to the strategic architecture and translated into activities and tasks that the workforce can understand. The selection of the CSFs should be based on the written vision and strategy of both the organization and the initiative in order to give the company the greatest leverage in a competitive environment.

Lower-level managers need to apply the input from senior management regarding CSFs within their operational units. First-level managers and individual contributors are best situated to identify the micro-level activities to satisfy the CSFs. The participation and support of these individuals is critical because they understand and do the work.

WHY? WHAT ARE THE BENEFITS?

Many initiatives become disjointed from the strategic direction and disconnected from the performance of the organization—they take on a life of their own. Clear CSFs provide a concise, logical linkage among the organization's goals, the initiative's goals, and individual contributors. The development of priorities, a part of setting CSFs, integrates the initiative with the strategic plan, reinforces the importance of the effort, and leads to the creation of objectives. It focuses employee efforts on activities that have measurable results.

The CSFs help overcome hurdles of lack of direction, of knowing what's important in implementation. They increase the organization's probability of success. Choosing only critical areas highlights what companies need to pay attention to during implementation.

Companywide involvement can be achieved by interlinking CSFs. Managers at each level include the level below them in participatory planning sessions. As a result people at each successive level have the initiative parameters they need. They are able to fill in the details of the plan, personalizing it to their type or level of responsibility while maintaining the strategic direction of the business through the CSFs.

HOW? A RECIPE FOR ACTION

After the architecture has been clearly defined (See Barrier 3: Lack of a planning architecture to guide the initiative), the organization needs to establish specific expectations, timelines, and outcomes. The priorities should close the gaps between current organization performance—in terms of customer satisfaction, financial metrics, market conditions, and product development—and the organization's richly envisioned future. The gap information needs to be cascaded throughout the organization and integrated into initiative activities that workgroups can address through concrete actions.

As a first step, a team can develop an overview that helps it to understand its role in achieving the initiative by tying it to the vision and the organization's CSFs. Table 1 presents a model that can be used for this high-level activity. The vision and CSFs will need to be supplied; the workgroup will apply these to the unit.

The workgroup can verify its contribution to the initiative by starting with its tasks and identifying the contribution to a CSF

TABLE 1

High-Level Alignment—Vision to Work Group

Our Vision—Company:		How the Initiative Links to the Vision
		What It Means to Our Unit:
Associated CSFs: ∎ ∎ ∎ ∎ ∎	Check those that apply to our unit:	How we impact/interact with the successful accomplishment of this particular CSF:

and then to the vision. Every task should tie in, or it should not be done. The grid in Table 2 is a tool to help with the associative process.

These tables are best filled in by the workgroup, including the manager. This allows for clarification, discussion, and public ownership of tasks.

WHO? IN WHAT MANNER?

Initiatives are most effective when the entire workforce becomes engaged and accountable for implementation.

Senior operational management determines the CSFs and allocates adequate resources to ensure that they are satisfied during initiative implementation.

Middle- and first-level management are responsible for deploying the initiative and managing the resources to enable the workgroups within their span of control to accomplish the tasks needed to satisfy their portion of the initiative.

The implementation team is responsible for maintaining an ongoing, two-way dialogue with managers and workgroups to ensure that the CSFs are clear, realistic, and achieved. They need to coordinate and collect data to guarantee that individual workgroup

TABLE 2

Critical Success Factor Activity Grid

Critical Success Factor—Detailed Definition				
What Specific Actions Are Needed to Ensure That We Satisfy Our Responsibility to This CSF?	Accountable Person(s) or Workgroup(s)	Support Function Person(s) or Workgroup(s)	Outcome (Results and Measurement)	Due Date

plans will accomplish the overall initiative objectives. The implementation team also is responsible for reviewing plans to ensure that they are coordinated with one another.

READING 9-1

A Fortune 500 company got rave reviews for its quality initiative because everyone in the organization understood how the initiative was interlocked and integrated into every aspect of its operations. This made it easy to track employee performance to the initiative's purpose and CSFs.

Lack of a Committed Leader—No One Is Willing to Take a Stand

BARRIER 10

	Preimplementation	During Implementation
Troubleshooting	✓	
Preventative Action		

Self-Assessment Questions

1. Does everyone know who is driving the initiative?
2. Is everyone is clear on how impassioned the leader is about the initiative?
3. Is there no question in anyone's mind as to what the leader is expecting from the improvement initiative?
4. Would people in the organization describe the leader as "larger than life"?

If You Answered No, Beware! Lack of clear articulation of business direction limits the organization's ability to focus on the future.

WHAT NEEDS TO BE DONE?

Every initiative must have a senior-level person who is committed and lets the organization know that "the train is going north"— either hop on to go north or hop off. This individual's role is to convey a strong mandate to everyone in the organization—from his or her direct reports to the mailroom clerk. The message is clear, consistent, and compelling. Because the individual is passionate about the importance of the initiative, she or he is able to:

- Explain the initiative to others.
- Provide examples of expected end results.·
- Generate enthusiasm in others.

True commitment begins with a big picture view that is communicated through a very public stand with the entire organization. Agreeing that an initiative is important, being a member of the design or implementation team, and/or writing a memo or two do not represent the requisite level of commitment. The committed leader must be able to "take the heat" or should not lead the process. This is especially important and difficult during the early phases of the initiative.

The leader is also responsible for challenging the organization to motivate individuals out of their sense of complacency and to recognize the importance of the initiative to change both processes and individual behaviors. This individual must aggressively act on opportunities that will bring about the change.

WHY? WHAT ARE THE BENEFITS?

Initiatives require people to change. The change process is difficult even for those who embrace it. When the leader articulates a clear direction and entices others to follow, the organization achieves the initiative as a unit. The committed leader engages the organization and asks it to assist in making the initiative a reality. Asking people to effect change in order to achieve an initiative's goals is dependent upon people:

- Clearly knowing who is asking them.
- Trusting the individual's conviction that the initiative will have a positive effect.

- Understanding precisely what they are being asked to do.
- Having been emotionally and intellectually swayed to the initiative's importance to the organization.

The leader's clarity on and decisiveness about the initiative limits "second guessing" about motives and expectations. It reduces the amount of speculation and the stress that is associated with uncertainty. People don't spend time trying to figure out what was meant; instead, they devote their energy to the initiative. People may not like the focus, but they understand the direction in which the organization is moving and are able to make a decision about their participation in the process.

HOW? A RECIPE FOR ACTION

A unique combination of traits are required to orchestrate the successful implementation of an initiative. A problem can arise if the chosen leader lacks these traits—they either do not exist in the person or are not dominant enough to provide the requisite leadership. The degree to which these traits exist within the leader will either foster or impede the initiative.

The scale in Table 1 identifies key characteristics that are present in committed leaders. Use it as a guide to rate your potential initiative leader. (You may wish to add other characteristics that are required by your particular initiative or organization.) The scale can help senior management identify a potential leader.

After reviewing your potential leader's attributes, evaluate his or her suitability for the role. Are characteristics missing or present only in limited degrees? Can these skills can be developed? If the proposed initiative is massive and the leader's characteristics are weak, the organization will need to reevaluate the situation. A lack of skill or ability in the key sponsor will impact the initiative's appeal to and acceptance by the workforce.

WHO? IN WHAT MANNER?

Involvement will depend upon the ability of the sponsoring source of the initiative.

TABLE 1

Leadership Commitment Characteristic Scale

Characteristic	Scale		
	Low		High
1. Able to dream out of the box.	1 2 3 4 5 6 7 8 9 10		
2. Unwillingness to give up on ideas that he or she believes in.	1 2 3 4 5 6 7 8 9 10		
3. Passionate, persistent, and consistent in telling their story.	1 2 3 4 5 6 7 8 9 10		
4. Has a high degree of self-confidence—permits hearing "no's" that lead to "yes."	1 2 3 4 5 6 7 8 9 10		
5. Open to feedback—see it as a tool for improvement not rejection.	1 2 3 4 5 6 7 8 9 10		
6. Action oriented.	1 2 3 4 5 6 7 8 9 10		
7. Willing to seek/accept help from others.	1 2 3 4 5 6 7 8 9 10		
8. Gives credit to others for their contributions.	1 2 3 4 5 6 7 8 9 10		
9. A good storyteller—engages people in the story so that they recognize the applicability of the message.	1 2 3 4 5 6 7 8 9 10		
10. Effective presenter—able to influence an audience.	1 2 3 4 5 6 7 8 9 10		

- If the initiative is the "dream" of a senior manager, involvement of others in determining leadership may be a moot point. If asked, others whom the leader trusts might act as sounding boards and advisers during the initiative's formative period. Ideally, they would have the power to influence/coach the leader.

- If the initiative is undertaken on behalf of an organization (the senior manager assigns someone to explore and introduce the initiative), the energizing leader can be appointed. In this situation, skill sets should be evaluated carefully.

The leader must be a risk taker—one who is courageous enough to stand up for the value of the initiative and make the hard decisions that will pave the way for its implementation. This individual also must be able to energize design team members, even when they get frustrated.

READING 10–1

A *Fortune* 100 leader believes that in a successful initiative the effective leaders create, demonstrate, personally own, and drive the initiative to completion.

The Organization's Lack of Readiness for the Initiative

	Preimplementation	During Implementation
Troubleshooting	✔	
Preventative Action		

Self-Assessment Questions

1. Are the people, resources, and climate supportive of the initiative?
2. Can you name at least three potential organizational barriers that can limit the initiative's success?
3. Can you identify behaviors within the organization that need to change to ensure effective implementation?
4. Have you positioned people to create and follow through on any action plans that might be developed to implement your initiative?

If You Answered No, Beware! The organization will be unable to address prerequisites, and thus cannot optimize the initiative.

WHAT NEEDS TO BE DONE?

The organization needs to evaluate its readiness for the initiative. Everything and everyone needs to be prepared, and systems must be put in place to ensure successful implementation. A part of the readiness process includes assessing how the endeavor will be accepted by the corporate culture. An assessment is an important first step because:

- It provides a picture of the organization and its members as a corporate entity.
- It evaluates the current state of the company and identifies the issues and challenges facing the initiative.
- It examines people's perceptions about the organization and the initiative.

Questions should focus on:

- Business needs.
- Communication.
- Leadership involvement.
- Barriers and other obstacles.

The data gathered helps to clarify what needs to be accomplished and what factors will help or hinder the ability to sustain initiative momentum.

WHY? WHAT ARE THE BENEFITS?

An organization that is thoroughly prepared to pursue its initiative stands a greater chance of success. The assessment process described in Table 1 is a "pre-test" that measures the organization's present state and provides a baseline against which the initiative can be compared as it unfolds. It is a strategic tool to stimulate thinking about what is and what can be, providing information about gaps, and it helps to prevents "solutions" being attempted that have little probability of acceptance.

The assessment results provide the organization's leadership with a factual basis for developing its implementation plan. The data can be drawn upon to support planning, communication, and maintenance. The results of the assessment will reveal strengths within the organization as well as indicate the resources that will be needed (whether in-house or to be recruited) for effective roll-out. The analysis highlights the organization's challenges and indicates priorities to focus on.

HOW? A RECIPE FOR ACTION

The relevant information is best gathered directly from people within the organization. The first question to be answered is, How extensively will we probe our staff? Will we:

- Poll everyone?
- Use sampling?
- Use focus groups (volunteer or randomly selected)?
- Rely upon the initiative team to provide the information, or gather information from other involved groups?

The size of the assessment target population will influence the format of the assessment, its questions, time requirements, support issues, team requirements, and whether internal or external resources are best to conduct the survey.

One technique that can be used to generate questions is to rely upon an assessment design team established for the sole purpose of determining readiness. They can brainstorm areas to identify readiness issues that need to be addressed. The areas generally fall into several generic categories (see Table 1).

A typical scenario for an internally developed assessment instrument would be:

1. The team reviews the categories to ensure that everyone shares a common definition of each category.
2. The group brainstorms potential questions.
3. The ideas are critiqued for applicability—how important is the information generated by these questions to determining readiness? (This is the point at which the scale on the right-hand side of the table is used.)
4. The final list of questions is agreed to by consensus; a sub-team reviews the questions for bias and clarity.

TABLE 1

Sample Readiness Assessment Instrument

Category	Question	Importance of Answering the Question to Initiative Rollout 1 = Low 5 = High
Business need	• How would you describe the initiative?	1 2 3 4 5
	• How would you describe the initiative's importance to the firm?	1 2 3 4 5
	• Do you feel that the company is going in the right direction by implementing the initiative? (Why/Why not?)	1 2 3 4 5
Communication	• What are your best sources of information?	1 2 3 4 5
	• Do you feel the organization keeps you informed about its improvement initiatives? (What can be done better?)	1 2 3 4 5
Leadership involvement	• Do senior managers adequately demonstrate their support for the initiative?	1 2 3 4 5
	• How committed is your manager toward the initiative?	1 2 3 4 5
	• What steps should the company take to demonstrate its commitment to integrating the endeavor into daily work?	1 2 3 4 5
Barriers/ impacts	• What obstacles need to be overcome for the initiative to be successful?	1 2 3 4 5
	• How do others in the firm view the initiative?	1 2 3 4 5
	• What is the biggest impact the initiative will have on work? on people?	1 2 3 4 5

   5. The survey is piloted (tested) with one cross-functional team to verify questions—do they collect the "correct" data?

Table 1 is a sample of a completed survey instrument. It can be assumed that each item carried an importance rating of a 3 minimum in order for it to be included in the final instrument.

WHO? IN WHAT MANNER?

The assessment design team needs to have contact with the entire organization. Everyone from mailroom clerks to senior managers contributes to the readiness of the organization for an improvement initiative and, therefore, the team needs to reflect all groups. Some organizations choose to create a representative team, others don't worry about full representation but concentrate instead on accurate data gathering. A random sample cross-section of the staff representing key operational areas and key levels should be interviewed, included on the team, or polled to elicit a wide range of workforce views.

Team members must be skilled at gathering unbiased information and be familiar with testing theory and practices. If members do not have the required skills, train them or use outside resources to provide expert advice.

READING 11–1

A service company conducted an internal assessment at several locations. The assessment captured how the organization currently operates and the knowledge and experience of its workforce relevant to the initiative. It identified what was important to the organization as well as some of the concerns regarding the initiative.

Managerial Tools Become Redundant

	Preimplementation	During Implementation
Troubleshooting		
Preventative Action	✓	

Self-Assessment Questions

1. Have initiative teams developed strategies to prevent an attitude of "this too shall pass" in employees when they introduce an improvement initiative?
2. Is your decision to introduce an improvement initiative and/or your selection of the managerial tool made logically by looking at the organization and its business needs?
3. Do initiative teams recognize that most endeavors flounder after six months to a year? Do you have a strategy in place to prevent dwindling support at this juncture?

If You Answered No, Beware! Employees won't relish or embrace the initiative as a personal and organizational competitive advantage.

WHAT NEEDS TO BE DONE?

A managerial tool is a technique, device, or approach that an organization can institute to improve operations. Examples include total quality management (TQM), benchmarking, high-performance teams, mass customization, economic value added, and business process reengineering. Decision makers assume that the currently touted managerial tool must be good because "everyone else is talking about it and using it." The assumption is that it will help the organization reach its goals—even if those goals have not been formulated or articulated. The reality is that a single managerial tool does not fit all situations. Initiative sponsors must avoid becoming so enamored of a particular tool (or consultant) that they arbitrarily select that tool to "fix" an organizational problem. It can also happen when top managers frequently change tools because a new one becomes popular.

Organizations must analytically and systematically evaluate a tool before selecting it and consider *why* they are implementing it. This process is key to gaining added economic value. When a company has a clear picture and purpose for the tool, it must evaluate if the implementation cost/effort will meet its needs. Questions that help to address this are:

1. Has the organization spent time to determine the root issue to be *solved* by the envisioned improvement tool?
2. Of the available tools, which will best achieve the expected outcomes and complement the organization's culture and strategy?

Too many organizations skip one or both of these questions and immediately select a tool without any up-front analysis. The key to avoiding this trap is to focus on problem resolution rather than on tool application.

WHY? WHAT ARE THE BENEFITS?

Businesses can be enhanced or inhibited by managerial tools, as shown in Table 1.

The key is to carefully assess and strategically implement choices. Employees begin to lose faith in the ability of the management team to effectively drive initiatives when poor choices are

TABLE 1

Enhancing and Inhibiting Characteristics of Managerial Tools

Characteristics of Problem-Resolution Focused Organizations	Characteristics of "Flavor-of-the-Month" Organizations
▪ Committed to "biting the bullet" in order to solve the problem right the first time. ▪ Seek the root cause of organizational problems to influence selection of the appropriate managerial tool. ▪ Outcomes are positive—employees openly engage in applying managerial tools when they are introduced.	▪ Don't have long-term strategies. ▪ Apply tools that promise a quick solution. ▪ Tools become Band-Aids and give the illusion that things are "fixed" when in fact they only addressed symptoms. ▪ Outcomes are ineffective—this creates distrust of future managerial tools that might be brought in.

made or when "good" choices are implemented poorly. Specifically impacted are:

The credibility of senior management. Employees begin to think about their limitations as leaders. Statements such as: "Don't they know what they want?" "How incompetent can they get?" and, "The new theory of the month is . . . " quickly begin to surface throughout the informal communication channels.

Employees' willingness to get involved. There is a feeling of "been there, done that"—people believed in and supported other tools and discovered they didn't make a long-term difference. They begin to take a removed attitude that says, "Show me it works then maybe I'll get involved (all the while thinking that this will probably disappear before my participation is required)."

Initiative facilitators lose their enthusiasm. The apathy affects those who are introducing the initiative. They don't understand why people can't realize the significance of the tool.

HOW? A RECIPE FOR ACTION

The first step in preventing a "flavor-of-the-month" mentality is to be clear about what the managerial tool should accomplish and what organizational issues it should solve. One technique is to rely on a sound problem-solving methodology. The organization needs to understand what is and is not working. This information should be the basis for identifying the best managerial tool to solve that specific problem. The process of tool selection includes asking questions to help the organization decide whether a tool will work within its environment. The number of potential tools to be evaluated will depend on the size and type of problem being resolved. Some problems by their nature are organizationwide, so few tools may be available for comparison. Others are more limited in scope, so several options can more easily be compared.

Table 2 provides sample criteria an organization might use to evaluate tools. Potential managerial tools can be listed in the horizontal column, and the criteria that must be considered by the organization can be listed in the columns at the left. The variables included in the matrix are generic to most evaluative processes but should not be considered all-inclusive.

The use of the matrix encourages an analytical evaluation and provides a visual representation of the best fit. Using a decision-table approach provides the initiative design team with concrete information that can be used throughout the process. A strong analytic basis gives more credence to the initiative because the "selling" points will be firm.

A NOTE OF CAUTION: Part of the decision-making process is recognizing that none of the evaluated tools may be the correct tool.

WHO? IN WHAT MANNER?

Different people/teams may be involved in each of the first two phases of the tool-selection process—uncovering the problem and selecting a managerial tool to resolve it. Typical participants include:

- Senior management.
- Other levels of management.
- Individual contributors.
- Internal or external consultants.
- Customer, supplier, and labor union partners.

Once the problem and its organizational impact have been determined, an appropriately positioned tool-selection team should be formed. Its task is to select the *right* managerial tool to address the problem at hand. Team participation will depend upon the particular problem.

TABLE 2

Managerial Tool Selection Matrix

| | Potential Tools | | | |
	Tool 1	Tool 2	Tool 3	Tool 4
How does the tool address the root issue?				
How closely does the tool match the organization's culture?				
Can we afford the effort/time to implement this tool? Is it worth it?				
Does it support other tools we've used? What are the links?				
What are the expected costs of implementing/not implementing?				
Are business drivers in place to support use of this tool?				
What are the risks of applying/ not applying this tool?				
What are management's expectations regarding the benefits of the tool?				

*Profits should be at least twice the cost to put the tool in place.

A NOTE OF CAUTION: A team that does not have the right mix of people—one that is too senior, missing critical stakeholders, or, conversely, is totally lacking management support, participation, or guidance—is unlikely to get to the root of the problem or select an effective tool.

READING 12–1

A high-tech organization in the throes of implementing a TQM program spent the first year training all 200 employees. In one of the sessions, a participant commented that this was simply "old wine in a new bottle." Unfortunately, most other employees agreed—and the initiative failed.

Lack of a Clear Rallying Point

	Preimplementation	During Implementation
Troubleshooting	✔	
Preventative Action		

Self-Assessment Questions

1. Is the make/break success factor of your initiative outside the organization—i.e., is the initiative's success beyond your control?
2. Does everyone in the organization know exactly why you must undertake the initiative regardless of its popularity or lack thereof?
3. Does everyone believe in the urgency of the initiative as a way of insuring the business's success, or perhaps even its existence?

If You Answered No, Beware! Employees won't be centered on a unified focal goal that activates all decisions and actions.

WHAT NEEDS TO BE DONE?

The organization needs to identify a focal rallying point for the improvement initiative if it is to succeed. A compelling rallying point will be quickly grasped by everyone in the organization. Everyone will support the initiative in order to meet the challenge of this force. In essence, the organization joins together to deal with the issue.

The rallying point is most powerful when it is outside the domain of those involved. The external focus becomes the impetus for initiating the change and the mirror in which all actions surrounding the initiative are reflected. It remains visible and reminds people to continue supporting the initiative.

WHY? WHAT ARE THE BENEFITS?

The focal point is the catalyst that motivates the organization to change. Initiatives without a rallying point frequently lose momentum and support after six months to a year. An issue critical enough to be a rallying point is usually urgent to the organization's survival/success. This makes it easier to garner the energy and commitment successful initiatives require. It creates a sense of "we against them" that generates enthusiasm and team unity. In such an environment, people are less likely to establish "turf."

One of the major hindrances to any improvement initiative is the inability to create a level of urgency surrounding the change. Pockets of people support the initiative; individuals align along political boundaries. Once these lines are drawn, they limit the success of the initiative because politics becomes more important than the initiative. Positioning the focal point outside the organization minimizes the lines and enables everyone to join together to deal with the external influence.

Some examples of the impact rallying points have had are shown in Table 1.

It may take much energy and planning, but an organization can create its own compelling, success-oriented rallying point. Examples of organizations that have done this well include Disney, Scandanavian Air Systems, and Federal Express.

TABLE 1

Impact of Rallying Points

Issue	Rallying Point	Rallying Point's Impact
▪ Drastic loss of customer base or market share due to unexpected performance by the competition	▪ Designed products and services that correlated to the needs of the customer	▪ Massive organizational change, which was guided by the initiative ▪ Used the initiative to look at ways to create products and services and identify improvement opportunities ▪ Elicited full adoption of the initiative and performance improved
▪ Going after customers' unmet needs	▪ "Speed, stretch targets, and boundaryless-turfless behavior." (Jack Welch, CEO of General Electric)	▪ Everyone in the organization sings from the same hymnal ▪ Considered to be a tough competitor within industries that they participate in ▪ Created leading-edge service solutions for customers' total business needs
	▪ Overnight delivery	▪ #1 in market ▪ Timely, reliable delivery for parcel services

HOW? A RECIPE FOR ACTION

To establish a rallying point, look to the operations or attitudes within the organization or to factors in the external environment. Pinpoint some entity that everyone in the organization can focus on. The greater the concern about the entity, the more likely the organization will wholeheartedly adopt the initiative.

How might this work? The key is to take an active stand. Most organizations know their weaknesses but don't want to give up comfortable habits and challenge operations. The leadership needs to be prepared to take an aggressive stand and create the desired need for change. Initiative cheerleaders can voice their support. They can also advertise the fact that the initiative fosters a more rewarding work environment.

If an organization determines that it does not have any critical weaknesses, it can create the need for a better future. Examples of issues that might be elevated into rallying points are shown in Table 2.

Once the issue and target group have been identified, a structured campaign around the initiative can be designed and implemented.

WHO? IN WHAT MANNER?

Identifying the rallying point and harnessing the energy of initiative participants is the responsibility of senior management. They are in a position to join the demands of the external force with the survival realities of the internal organization.

Employees must become involved and accept the challenge presented by the rallying point. Roles and contributions differ, but the measure of an effective rallying point is that it energizes and motivates everyone to action focused on achieving the initiative's goals.

READING 13–1

A health maintenance organization found that its backroom operations were limiting its ability to compete. The organization determined the per claim processing costs that would have to be met because "best practices" firms were setting those standards for the industry. Everyone in the organization understood the dollar reductions that were required, and they knew that failing to meet the standards would mean the end of the organization. This clear focus energized employees to do all those things that were required to meet the clearly understood goals.

TABLE 2

Examples of Potential Rallying Points

Type of Organization	Issue That Could Be Converted into a Focal Point	Potential External Rallying Points
▪ Financial services	▪ Changes in competition base driven by revised government regulations	▪ New product developers ▪ Economic value added ▪ New distribution channels
▪ Educational institution	▪ Tuition vouchers	▪ Parents ▪ Legislature

No Marketing Strategy to Recruit Appropriate Support

	Preimplementation	During Implementation
Troubleshooting		
Preventative Action	✓	

Self-Assessment Questions

1. Are there necessary and sufficient activities in place to promote the initiative?
2. Are there people in the organization who are capable of applying marketing strategies to the initiative?
3. Is marketing part of the strategic plan for the initiative?

If You Answered No, Beware! The power of the initiative to influence change is diminished because the organization doesn't optimally market its significance to the workforce.

WHAT NEEDS TO BE DONE?

To be successful, an improvement initiative must be guided by a clear marketing strategy. One outcome of the strategy is to sell the initiative to the implementation team, the organization at large, and, if large-scale enough, to the customer community.

Key questions that need to be asked are:

- Is the organization crystal clear on the value the initiative will offer to the organization? To the target groups? To outside audiences?
- What distribution channels will you use to market the initiative?
- How can you capitalize on word-of-mouth to inform associates about the benefits of the initiative?
- How can you halt declining support for the initiative?
- Do you need different marketing strategies for each group?

Too often, organizations place the marketing strategy further down in the planning process and it becomes a hit-and-miss activity. Effective marketing assumes that the organization determines *what* actions are needed and establishes the timetable for those actions. Only at that point can the organization begin to think about *who* will be involved.

The organization's initiative planners need to target, attract, and gain acceptance from employees. They should begin by profiling those who will be recruited to do the marketing and those to whom the initiative is being marketed. This will clarify the needs of the various targeted groups, the availability of resources to accommodate those demands, and the best strategy to tap resources to further the initiative.

Organizations can adopt a public relations (PR) mindset as a technique to effectively market a proposed initiative. If the organization balks at putting energy into this up-front marketing task, it probably isn't totally committed to the initiative itself—consider this a warning to step back and rethink the viability of the initiative.

WHY? WHAT ARE THE BENEFITS?

Marketing presents the sponsors' explanation of the value of the initiative to members of the organization in a way that will rally them to the cause. Through marketing the sellers of the initiative create a demand for it in the targeted audience. An initiative that doesn't garner the proper up-front support is doomed to failure. It is more difficult to gain support and loyalty for the initiative than it is to lose it. The steps to market the initiative are:

- Align the message with the various constituencies.
- Get people involved and enthused by selling the initiative to the organization at large, tying it to business value.
- Spell out the actions required by various groups, at various times—provide templates to make action easy.

Organizations that assume that the inherent "goodness" of the initiative will be seen, understood, and embraced by those who have been targeted without any concerted marketing effort are naive. "Goodness" is defined by each person; thus, the initiative's benefits must be incorporated into a marketing strategy that will encourage employees to redirect their energy toward the goals of the endeavor.

HOW? A RECIPE FOR ACTION

Marketing an initiative helps individuals in the organization understand the total cost/benefit consequences of supporting the endeavor. Variables to consider in order to target and then address different segments include:

- Dividing the organization into market segments—define and profile each.
- Looking at what has worked historically with each group.
- Understanding the business from the targeted group's perspective.
- Understanding the threats that this initiative poses for each segment.
- Determining the bargaining power and weight that different segments have to potentially influence the initiative.

- Looking for other organizational efforts that will compete with the initiative.

The marketing strategy must be built upon a clear knowledge of the targeted audience. It is generally not a single body. Build profiles of each group; think in terms of the subgroups: what are they like, what would make the initiative worthwhile for each group, and how best to reach them? Although the message sent throughout the organization must be uniform, the packaging need not be the same. Oral or written, serious or light, from senior officers or team members, use various presentation options to elicit support for the message from different audiences.

To gain an understanding of the marketing needs of a particular audience, think in terms of elements that impact how a group will react to the initiative based on these variables. Use the matrix in Table 1 to first identify specific market segments/audiences found in your organization (enter one in each of the blank columns). Then answer each of the questions on the left as regards a particular segment (these are a guide—you can add more information based on the situation in your organization).

WHO? IN WHAT MANNER?

Generally designing the overall marketing strategy is the responsibility of individuals at a senior level who are able to grasp the big picture. A skill required, whether drawn from the senior group or provided by a specialized marketing/PR person, is understanding how to market to any target audience.

To find the requisite people, use the steps below as a guide. Notice that identifying the specific person is only addressed after the business needs have been considered. The least important issue should be availability—if the initiative is important, key people should be freed up to participate in it.

1. What are the personal traits and technical skills required of individuals who are going to map out and then address the marketing strategy?
2. Who in the organization possesses the traits?
3. How do you free them up to take on the marketing role?
4. Do you need outside resources to help develop marketing strategy?

TABLE 1

Evaluation of Needs of Various Targeted Market Segments

	Targeted Market Segment			
Element	**Segment 1**	**Segment 2**	**Segment 3**	**Segment 4**
1. What features of the initiative will each segment value?				
2. When should the initiative be shared with that market segment?				
3. How do we organize the marketing efforts to reach this particular segment?				
4. What resources need to be allocated?				
5. What are the time frames to market during each stage* of initiative adoption?				
6. What are the hurdles that will impact the marketing strategy?				

*Initiative stages are design, implementation, maintenance, and shutdown.

COMMUNICATION

The Rhythm of the Organization

	Preimplementation	During Implementation
Troubleshooting	19. Not understanding that everyone wants to know: What's in it for me? 22. Inability to harness the informal communication channels.	17. Saturation of communication— all talk and no action. 18. Inconsistent communication results in mixed messages. 23. Not measuring the effectiveness of internal communication. 24. The predicament of making mistakes.
Preventative Action	15. The blind leading the blind. 20. Inefficiency of not learning the lessons.	16. People lack communication skills. 21. Lack of *open* communication.

Within organizations, numerous messages are passed from one individual to another. For initiative communication to be effectual, one must understand what it is and why it is an enhancer or inhibitor. Communication transfers information to others via memos, in person, through meetings, and through electronic media. It can be either formal or informal. Effective communication is *goal directed*; that is, the message has a specific purpose and effect on the recipient. Inefficient communication occurs when messages convey a meaning different than intended or when they are obstructed. Potential barriers to communication discussed in this section include:

- Unreliable information.
- Lack of credibility of the person transmitting the message.
- Individual differences and perceptions of the meaning of the message.
- Doubts about messages or media because of past experiences.
- Uneven distribution of information.
- Lack of accessibility to necessary information.

A communication strategy addressing messages to be transmitted as well as potential barriers serves to keep the communication on track. It provides a foundation for managing initiative information on a daily basis and ensures that the communication is reliable, consistent, and proper for the various audiences within the company. Initiative communication planners assess the population, determine the benefits of the endeavor to specific targeted groups, and orchestrate the words and media accordingly.

Comprehensive evaluation of the strategy is essential to guarantee that information is open and timely and that messages are sent and received as planned. The review also determines how well the organization created opportunities for employees to discuss their fears and concerns about the endeavor. An open forum addresses concerns in a rational, logical manner, which can further the adoption of the effort.

The Blind Leading the Blind

	Preimplementation	During Implementation
Troubleshooting		
Preventative Action	✓	

Self-Assessment Questions

1. Can the leaders of the initiative spell out its purpose in 25 words (two sentences) or less?
2. Do the leaders have a clear expectation of what the initiative will bring to the organization?
3. Do the messages conveyed by senior managers about the initiative prevent confusion and misunderstanding?
4. Are your sponsors open individuals who are willing to receive feedback?

If You Answered No, Beware! Lack of clarity and purpose at the top means no one knows what the initiative can accomplish.

WHAT NEEDS TO BE DONE?

We ask employees to accept an initiative on a blind leap of faith. The success of the initiative is based on how well the company's leaders understand and communicate it. Executive management needs to have clear expectations and communicate them well so that everyone can see where the organization is headed.

Too often, *leaders of* the initiative may not have any clearer picture of the what's and why's of the initiative than do the followers. Typical examples of this suboptimum knowledge being communicated include:

- Use of inaccurate terms to describe the process and the initiative.
- Untruths and half-truths (generally from ignorance) that mislead the workforce.
- A shutdown of communication as a way of obscuring a lack of understanding.
- An aura of secrecy about the initiative—"when you have had training you will understand what I'm talking about."
- Inappropriate communication techniques to denigrate questions that others raise in their attempt to understand and assimilate the initiative.

WHY? WHAT ARE THE BENEFITS?

When those responsible for driving the initiative don't understand it, they miscommunicate it to others in the organization. Clearly communicated views help employees see the value and benefit of the initiative, and thus encourage them to buy in to the process even before substantive evidence of initiative results can be seen. Poorly communicated messages present smoke screens that often hide a lack of knowledge or communication skills. Employees sense or see through these smoke screens and refuse to actively and fully support the initiative.

Preventing or correcting inadequate communication is important because of the damage it can do to the initiative. Early communications must be clear, accurate, and informative. One impediment initiative designers may face in their attempts to clarify and correct sponsors' early communications is the person's hierarchical position. It becomes a highly sensitive and political issue if the senior person is unwilling to hear feedback about his or her (mis)understanding of the initiative.

HOW? A RECIPE FOR ACTION

A goal of a communication strategy is to insure that the sponsor and other key players:

- Accurately and thoroughly understand and define expectations for the initiative.
- Are articulate in describing expectations and strategy to others.
- Are willing to seek out and listen to feedback to test their understanding of the initiative.

Some techniques that can be used to educate senior management to prevent their "blindly" leading the initiative include:

- Provide scripts and/or bullet points for senior managers to reference when they provide information regarding the initiative.
- Be prepared to make very clear to your senior managers what you want them to cover in presentations and the messages you want to send to the audience. Put it in writing if possible.
- Be willing to provide preparatory sessions for the senior managers during which potential audience questions and concerns can be identified ahead of time. Senior managers will then know the issues and can answer questions in a way that employees will find convincing.
- Help these individuals modify their messages when feedback indicates that employees didn't understand presented information.
- Specifically schedule time for senior management "town meetings"/information sessions to occur.

Blindness is eradicated when senior managers are willing to listen
to messages about their communication.

WHO? IN WHAT MANNER?

Dealing with senior managers is always a sensitive issue in any
organization. The individuals who help prevent blindness in
senior managers must possess a great deal of self-confidence and
have a strong belief in the importance of the initiative to the organization's well-being. Desirable characteristics in those who educate senior managers to understand and communicate the
initiative throughout the organization include:

- Creditability and the respect of senior managers. Recognize
  that in some organizations this position can only be filled
  by outside consultants.
- Ability to fulfill the role of process leader, well-versed in all
  aspects of the initiative, and able to share their knowledge.
- Willingness to operate outside the box.
- Willing to bear the repercussions that come when operating
  outside the box (including being the bearer of bad news to a
  senior manager who won't like hearing it).

READING 15–1

A medical services provider initiated a very successful redesign effort.
The key to its effectiveness was the CEO's complete understanding of
what needed to be in place to make such a process a success. Because of
this knowledge communication was clear and frequent. As a result, key
resources were assigned full time to the process. Implementation dates
were established only when it was clear they could be met. Drastic
changes were permitted. The firm was committed to including all
impacted groups, so that multiple points of view could be incorporated.

People Lack Communication Skills

	Preimplementation	During Implementation
Troubleshooting		
Preventative Action		✔

Self-Assessment Questions

1. Have you assessed the communication skills of your target audiences?
2. Have individuals received feedback about their one- and two-way communications?
3. Do the leaders of the initiative constantly practice effective communication and thus act as role models for others in the organization?
4. Do you provide a variety of mechanisms (inside and outside the work unit) that encourage employees to develop their communication skills?

If You Answered No, Beware! The organization will fall short of gaining the maximum return for its time spent in communication.

WHAT NEEDS TO BE DONE?

What constitutes successful communication? If asked, most leaders will indicate they have the skill to communicate effectively. However, statistics from both successful and failed initiatives suggest that few really possess the necessary communication skill level to get messages across. Competency includes the ability to use communications as a tool to help the organization take ownership of the initiative; it is not simply the ability to talk to a group of employees.

Initiative designers need to conduct a reality check to accurately profile the skill level of those responsible for promoting change. In actuality there are few people who are dynamic enough communicators to gain mass support for an organizational change. If skill is lacking, the designers will need to:

- Rethink or rescale the initiative.
- Recruit "better" communicators.
- Develop different communication strategies that are more compatible with available personnel.

WHY? WHAT ARE THE BENEFITS?

Communication allows individuals to send messages throughout the organization. People typically spend anywhere from 45 to 75% of their work time communicating with others. During times of change, much of this interaction focuses on communicating what is wanted/expected in the changed organization. Having individuals in place who are capable of promoting an initiative will motivate the workforce to a higher level of both engagement and risk taking. Simply *reciting* an initiative's message will not instill ownership.

The skill level of those publicly communicating the initiative will either inhibit or enhance dispersion and adoption. It is the responsibility of the sponsors of the initiative to ensure that skills sets are commensurate with the scope of the endeavor. Asking a person with mid-range skills to drive an initiative that impacts many thousands of people will doom it to failure.

HOW? A RECIPE FOR ACTION

Communication is a basic competency. Leaders must be clear on the messages that they are responsible for sending and understand how they may be received. Ongoing feedback is required to evaluate how well leaders are shaping employee perceptions about the initiative. An assessment of leaders' communication abilities to accurately transmit messages and generate a positive response must be completed at the time leaders are recruited.

An effective technique for identifying competencies is the force field analysis. This tool can help to reveal those variables that support or hinder the ability of the communicators to persuade the organization of the initiative's merit. The organization's leaders and key communicators need to identify the elements of the competencies that will inhibit or enhance its success. It may require expert assistance to identify the elements specific to the organization. Two examples of elements associated with communication competency are shown in Table 1. In the left column are examples of cognitive communication skills. The right column provides examples of affective skills.

TABLE 1

Communication Competencies

Technical Communication Skills	Influencing Skills
▪ Ability to use body language to further the message. ▪ Charisma. ▪ Ability to speak in a "language" and at a level that the audience can relate to; attuned to audience vernacular. ▪ Excellent command of the language—able to use exactly the right word, phrasing statement in exactly the right way. ▪ Mastery of one's own voice—tone, volume, modulation, etc. ▪ Pulls the audience into the communication.	▪ Respected for both personal integrity and technical knowledge. ▪ Has an aura of success—the person's project will work. ▪ Obsessed with and passionate about the initiative. ▪ Able to move others to new ground even if it is "unsafe." ▪ High levels of energy. ▪ Demonstrated confidence in an ability to make the initiative happen.

The next step is to determine those who currently posses the critical competencies and those who lack them but might benefit from training.

If gaps are identified, a decision will need to be made:

- Is the skill present somewhere in the organization, and can we recruit internally?
- If the skill is totally lacking, should the initiative be refocused, rescaled, or shelved.

The critical factor is to align an individual's responsibility within the initiative to the level of skill competency.

The model in Table 2 can be used as a brainstorming tool by an organization trying to identify supports and barriers to competencies. The importance rating should be a driving factor determining the amount of energy and resources applied to the particular element. The level of skill and energy devoted to training and recruitment also needs to be aligned with the importance rating.

WHO? IN WHAT MANNER?

Changing communication patterns requires support from senior executives. Senior management needs to understand the importance of effective communication to the initiative and be willing to support the effort by providing adequate resources for the development of these skills.

Individuals who are skilled in the art of communication need to be included in the process to help identify those in the organization who should communicate the initiative's message. They may be the preferred communicators themselves, or they may serve as role models.

TABLE 2

Assessment of Critical Communication Competencies

Specific Communication Competency	What Makes This Competency an Enhancer?	What Makes This Competency an Inhibitor?*	Importance of the Identified Element to Overall Competency	Who Is Currently Skilled in the Competency?	Who Would Benefit From Skills Training?	Others in the Organization Who Might Be Recruited

*Look for ways to minimize inhibitors or convert them to enhancers.

79

Saturation of Communication—All Talk and No Action

	Preimplementation	During Implementation
Troubleshooting		✓
Preventative Action		

Self-Assessment Questions

1. Does your communication style avoid "hype" words—i.e., super-latives without behavioral or concrete ties?
2. Have you calculated the ratio of talk to action messages associated with any initiative?
3. Have you assessed the effectiveness of your communication strategy in terms of credibility as regards commitment to action?

If You Answered No, Beware! Your efforts at communication will yield no concrete, results-focused messages, and employees will lose interest in the initiative.

WHAT NEEDS TO BE DONE?

People who are asked to participate in or adopt any initiative want to know that they will see action as well as hear speeches. It is the responsibility of the sponsoring group to design a systematic and logical flow to communicating the initiative. Planning is the tool that ensures that communication is more than just talk. Communication is facilitated when people recognize the tangible value of the initiative. The organization is responsible for a plan of action supporting the initiative that will lead to early value-added outcomes and accomplishments.

WHY? WHAT ARE THE BENEFITS?

Action-oriented communication ensures that everyone understands the purpose and phasing of the initiative and that energy is focused and expended appropriately. Many organizations have been through numerous changes; people know that the process of achieving the envisioned future described by the initiative will be painful. Therefore, most individuals want proof that the struggle will result in concrete benefits to both themselves and their organization.

Employees look for ways to verify that the initiative is driving the organization's actions and decisions. When people continue to hear about the benefits of an initiative but never see tangible results or actions, they lose interest. They see the initiative and its supporters as lacking credibility and are thus unwilling to support the endeavor.

The communication planners must provide hard evidence because:

- We live in a media age in which people are accustomed to slick presentations. To make the initiative more than a "soapbox presentation," its sponsors must plan for specific actions that are directly tied to results.
- Today's organizations are flatter, and people are becoming leery of taking on tasks that are outside of their immediate job responsibility. They fear that getting involved with an initiative that hasn't demonstrated substantive actions will

result in wasted efforts, or that they will end up being at the "bleeding edge" of the initiative.

HOW? A RECIPE FOR ACTION

The goal of the communication plan is to develop concrete messages that link talk to results or attainable goals.

- Determine the initiative's milestones and expected outcomes.
- At every phase, align the communication script with concrete results that can be achieved. The value of the initiative is measured in terms of perceptions of its practicality and ability to deliver on promises as outlined in the milestones.

> Gantt charts are frequently used for this purpose. They lay out milestones for various phases/tasks associated with an initiative and provide a graphic rendering of the project's progress.

Table 1 provides a general guide and highlights points that those responsible for communication planning must consider and align.

Using the matrix will ensure that messages are tied to specific milestones or stages of the initiative. Relying on a logical matrix approach prevents communication from becoming chaotic and protects it from the whims of those in charge.

WHO? IN WHAT MANNER?

It is the responsibility of the initiative sponsor, project leader, team members responsible for communications planning, and communications expert to align project goals, communications, and actionable outcomes. Those selected for this task must understand the initiative and the culture and be able to communicate it in action-oriented ways that will motivate the audience.

Individuals accountable for this task must be sensitive to issues such as:

- Cultural differences.

TABLE 1

Communication Script Assessment Matrix

Initiative Milestone	Associated Communication Script	Points to Help the Target Audience Associate the Message in the Script to Actions	Ratio of Generalities to Specific Action Statements or Outcomes			Measures to Determine Whether People Perceive the Initiative to Be Actionable
			Number of Generalities	Number of Specific Action Statements	Ratio*	

*An 80-20 ratio of specific action statements to generalities will provide concrete direction to the initiative's messages.

- Understanding nuances of words used in the communications.
- Sophistication of the audiences.
- Global issues faced by international organizations.
- Personal values and expectations of the various affected groups.

Sensitivity is critical because every person responsible for communication has the power to influence perceptions of the organization as one that acts as well as talks.

Inconsistent Communication Results in Mixed Messages

	Preimplementation	During Implementation
Troubleshooting		✔
Preventative Action		

Self-Assessment Questions

1. Do you have a central point for all initiative communication—one person or unit having final say regarding messages that are going out?
2. Can you identify communication vehicles, and are you tapping into the most effective ones?
3. Do you avoid an attitude of "on an as-needed-basis" in communicating with various business units?
4. Do you periodically check your communication plan for clarity and refocus it as necessary?

If You Answered No, Beware! Employees don't trust what they hear about the initiative because different organizational units are hearing different messages.

WHAT NEEDS TO BE DONE?

An organization must be uniform in the messages it conveys to various employee units. There must be consistency among all the communication channels—written, face-to-face, and remote. People in different functional units and at different levels need to hear a common message. This is key to gaining support for the improvement initiative.

The organization walks a fine line in maintaining consistency and accommodating individual differences. Everyone needs to hear a uniform message; however, they may not all favor the same medium. Communication planners must figure out how to ensure that different groups will all *hear* the *same message* at the same time through the different media.

> A NOTE OF CAUTION: Making such accommodations can raise certain dangers:
>
> - Different messages end up going to different groups.
> - Messages passed down through layers of the organization result in the "telephone game," which produces diluted and/or garbled information.

Senior managers' role in the communication process is to ensure that everyone hears and understands the importance and urgency of the initiative to the success of the organization. To be effective, their message must focus on the specific actions employees must take to achieve the initiative's goals. The message must elicit a call for action. A central person or team should ensure that everyone responsible for the initiative's communication is in alignment and presents one uniform message.

WHY? WHAT ARE THE BENEFITS?

Consistent communication is not an easy task for any firm; however the benefits are a collective direction, clear signals, and an increased respect from both workforce and customers. It serves as a guide, keeps the initiative on track, and provides a foundation for managing the initiative's information on a day-to-day basis.

An uneven spread of information can lead to isolation and secrecy among and within workgroups, which causes counterproductivity—energy goes into finding out what others know or into speculating about the message, and this takes effort away from constructive action. Allowing different messages (in terms of content, format, or completeness) results in employees questioning the strategy of the initiative itself and the credibility of those sending the messages. When messages differ, people tend to create information to fill the void or rely upon the informal channels found in all organizations. (See Barrier: Inability to harness the informal communication channels.)

Conflict between what the firm says the initiative should do and what it actually accomplishes leads to negative employee perceptions. Inconsistent communication can result in people assuming that there are cliques within the organization comprised of those who know and those who don't know. This inhibits openness and can impact future information sharing. The initiative needs to be fully understood and openly discussed. Any fears that employees might harbor need to be brought to the surface and resolved.

HOW? A RECIPE FOR ACTION

The initial step in the process is to assemble the appropriate people and develop the communication plan. Typical elements that might be included in such a plan are:

1. Determining the options that the organization traditionally relies upon within each of the media categories. (Table 1 lists commonly utilized media.)

2. Creating a communications timeline: What needs to be communicated, how often, and when? The goal is to ensure balance in terms of message intervals and a variety of media.

3. Testing media options to ensure that those selected are appropriate for the messages being sent and that they ensure uniformity. Are people hearing what was intended?

4. Assessing resource requirements: How much and who? When selecting individuals, consider their position within the organization and the respect they command from the workforce.

TABLE 1

Common Types of Communications Media

Written	Face-to-Face	Remote
▪ Newsletters. ▪ Bulletin boards. ▪ Flyers. ▪ Annual report. ▪ Electronic messaging. ▪ Communication resource manual for managers.	▪ Scripted meeting. ▪ Roundtables. ▪ Breakfasts (generally with senior managers). ▪ Department meetings. ▪ All-employee meetings.	▪ State-of-the business update by the senior manager. ▪ Multisite video sessions. ▪ Videotapes.

5. Accounting for organizational differences. This can be driven by the global nature of the business/locations/operational units. It can also be driven by internal diversity of workers.

6. Addressing the commonly asked questions through use of various formats, preferably interactive.

A Q & A guide such as the one shown in Table 2 can help the communication team map out the information required for the plan.

WHO? IN WHAT MANNER?

The communicators must have a complete understanding of the initiative and its impact on the organization. They need knowledge, credibility, and the sensitivity required to understand various audiences and their needs. Individuals skilled in evaluation and measurement should be included on the communication team to determine the effectiveness of the messages sent and received.

TABLE 2

Communication Q & A Planning Guide

Questions to Address for Communication Planning	Organization's Response—What Has Been Done, or Will Be Done, to Address the Item?
1. What to say?	
2. Why does it need to be said?	
3. Who needs to hear it?	
4. Who is best positioned to say it?	
5. What media are best to convey the message to meet the needs of the targeted audience?	
6. How should current media be modified to support the initiative?	
7. When should the message be conveyed?	
8. How often should the message be conveyed?	
9. Did recipients receive the message in the way it was intended?	
10. How is the effectiveness of the message to be measured?	

Not Understanding That Everyone Wants to Know: What's in It for Me?

	Preimplementation	During Implementation
Troubleshooting	✔	
Preventative Action		

Self-Assessment Questions

1. Can you identify the various cultural groups within the organization?
2. Do you regularly use different approaches to communicate messages to different audiences?
3. Are you sensitive to the needs of the various audiences affected by the initiative?
4. Are multiple sources available through which people can get answers about the initiative?
5. Do communication planners understand that different people need different information about the initiative at different points in the roll-out cycle?

If You Answered No, Beware! Messages that are not targeted to specific needs of individuals or groups result in either too little action or too much reaction.

WHAT NEEDS TO BE DONE?

People are driven by different motivators—the *What's In It For Me?* (WIIFM) syndrome—and these vary for each person or work-group. Successfully communicated initiatives provide a range of information about the endeavor that meets the needs of everyone affected. The communication process targets specific audiences and influences their attitudes and behaviors. People will support an initiative most readily when they see a direct association between participating in the initiative and satisfying their own needs. Designers must take the time to determine the recipients' orientation, so that messages can be tailored to their needs.

The goal is to align initiative benefits so that communication focuses on business unit or personal objectives that will motivate individuals to action. It requires taking the time to determine the appropriate medium—that is, what medium works best with what audience?

Information sequencing must support its pertinence to the group. How will it leverage the group's performance? Understanding the WIIFM syndrome allows effective communication strategies to be developed and executed.

> For example, people who must be on the telephone all day don't have time to attend meetings to watch a video and then discuss it. Instead they could find time between calls to read a brief bulletin or a message in the electronic messaging system. (If a video is considered a "must-see," make it available for take-home viewing.)

WHY? WHAT ARE THE BENEFITS?

Messages have not been communicated until they have been *received* and *accepted*. In today's busy workplace, people get over-loaded and aren't willing to spend the time to figure out how specific messages relate to their environments and jobs. When they can't readily determine the collective purpose of how the initiative applies to their specific job, they ignore it.

Individuals are motivated to adopt and implement the endeavor when they recognize its value to themselves. This is the outcome of identifying and satisfying the question, What is in it for me? It is the job of the initiative designers to communicate a clear picture of initiative results and personal/work unit benefit.

HOW? A RECIPE FOR ACTION

A key to successfully determining WIIFMs is to anticipate what a recipient wants to hear. By working backwards, planners can understand what each group will respond and commit to and then develop communications to meet those needs and expectations.

Before communication can be targeted to audiences, the organization must find some way of categorizing employees into logical groupings. Some considerations that will influence this segmentation and the nature of probable questions each group will pose include:

- Determine the degree of impact the initiative will have on groups or individuals—this influences the amount of information that must be shared. The greater the degree of impact, the greater the information need.
- Look at roll-out plans and identify those who will be exposed first to the initiative. The closer to implementation a group is, the more pressing its need to learn about the initiative—its process and impact on the individuals involved.
- Look at the professional and personality profiles of people in various areas—people with certain skills tend to populate certain fields, and this can influence communication (e.g., engineers and actuaries will not want to hear the same form of message as will sales and human resource staff).

Questions that people will typically ask when informed about a new endeavor include:

- How will this impact me?
- Will this take more work?
- How will it make a difference to my work and how I do it?

Initiative designers need to brainstorm probable questions in light of the various populations within their organization. Use the matrix shown in Table 1 as a guide for your planning.

TABLE 1

Question Planning Guide

Group	Their Motivators and Concerns	Probable Questions	Potential Answers to Demonstrate Initiative Value and Gain Commitment

Once the groups have been identified and potential questions planned for:

- Tie the information about the initiative to the business orientation and interests of each audience. Use appropriate jargon so that people hear, relate to, and can act upon messages. This requires knowing the types and formats of information that work units or cultural groups trust and respond to.

- Choose the best people based on their ability to interact with each group. The people who communicate are equally as important as the message itself.

- Focus on how the WIIFM syndrome motivates each group. Care must be taken to ensure that the messages are not condescending or insensitive, which would negatively affect the communication.

The next step is to identify the appropriate tool for the communication. The best strategy is to encourage face-to-face communication between management and employee groups. The goal is to encourage an open exchange about the initiative, to air issues. The value of such forums is that managers can address the specific concerns and interests of those in attendance. Given today's dispersed workgroups, face-to-face interaction is not always possible. Other forums for two-way communication that can accommodate geographic dispersion need to be included in the initiative's communication plan. Examples of ways this communication can take place are shown in Table 2.

TABLE 2

Highly Interactive Forms of Communication

On-Site, Face-to-Face Sessions	Dispersed, Two-Way Interaction
▪ Monthly rap sessions. ▪ Town meetings. ▪ Roundtable discussions. ▪ Focus groups.	▪ Video or audio conferencing. ▪ Satellite broadcasts with call-in. ▪ A variation of a help line—a toll free number that anyone can call with questions and get a live answer. ▪ Internet or e-mail address (electronic bulletin boards).

WHO? IN WHAT MANNER?

The person guiding the communication process needs a comprehensive view of the organization and must be sensitive to the various employee groups. This may require outside consultants who are experienced in assessing organizations and arranging employees into logical communication groupings.

Individuals who conduct the communication sessions need to be perceived by the group as having the right combination of control, respect, and support. Based upon the organization's staff, culture, and resources the sessions can be conducted by a project team member who is knowledgeable about the initiative; a manager (preferably not immediate; instead, recruit an individual who is at least one level above or is lateral); the consultant; and/or as human resources person who is well-versed with change management.

READING 19–1

An aerospace firm uses videotapes as a way of communicating quarterly updates. These are sent to employees' homes so that all family members can learn about the organization's activities. The opportunity to watch the videotapes at home encourages employees to take the time to view them. They involve family members in the viewing process and builds support with the family for the "extra hours" that employees are frequently required to work.

Inefficiency of Not Learning the Lessons

	Preimplementation	During Implementation
Troubleshooting		
Preventative Action	✓	

Self-Assessment Questions

1. Is there documentation of communication strategies from past initiatives?
2. Is there a history of effective communication to support past initiatives?
3. Do you document a history of communication effectiveness from a variety of audiences within the organization?

If You Answered No, Beware! Repeating past errors results in deterioration in credibility of the initiative and management.

WHAT NEEDS TO BE DONE?

Many companies invest time, energy, and resources to design communication plans for an initiative without accessing information from previous efforts. A plan needs to be in place to ensure that accurate documentation is mandated for all initiatives. Evaluations of past communication strategies and tactical plans need to be referenced. The goal is to develop a rich history of the organization's communication methods—for both past and current initiatives—and use the information to manage future communication.

The type of data collected and the questions asked will be different for a historical perspective (studying the effects of a past initiative) than for a formative evaluation (using collected data to influence current operations). It requires going beyond a superficial look at communication to an examination of how previous strategies and plans worked or didn't work. Communication planners need to consider the impact of the previous initiatives on various recipients. The organization's communication flow needs to be dissected by horizontal, vertical, functional, and organizational levels as well as geographic location to obtain an accurate picture.

WHY? WHAT ARE THE BENEFITS?

Successful initiatives include data that evaluates previous localized, focused communication targeted to people, media, and content. This increases both receptivity to the message and employee willingness to support the initiative.

The use of summary and formative evaluation approaches allows the organization to develop a depth of understanding regarding the communication process within the organization. Evaluation identifies those conditions/elements that can be incorporated into the strategy for the current, planned initiative. It supplies data so that past mistakes can be avoided in the current initiative.

People will think positively about an initiative's communications when:

- They are asked about its effectiveness.
- They see the information incorporated into future communications, messages, and media selection.

- They see initiative planners taking action upon feedback. This makes a statement as to the worthiness of the information and the communicators.

HOW? A RECIPE FOR ACTION

Begin by seeking historical information (this can be written or oral). This will recount the communication strategy and media used with past initiatives. The information gatherers should be asking questions such as those shown in Table 1.

Bring a team together to analyze the information and develop or update a communication strategy that incorporates past and

TABLE 1

Guide for Historical Information Gathering

Medium Being Assessed			
	Responses by Audience Group		
Questions	Group 1	Group 2	Group 3
What is the profile? Include: - Group descriptions - Content of message - Frequency of contact			
How did specific audiences react to the medium?			
Were implementation ideas proposed for the medium that weren't tapped into, but that in hindsight should have been tried?			
What media are currently being used with the group? Rate their degree of success.			
Is there feedback (solicited/ unsolicited) that needs to be incorporated into future planning of media selection?			

current lessons. Be sure to provide feedback to the work units as to how their input was incorporated.

A quick checklist for developing communications should include the following:

- Ensure the communication plan matches the stage of the initiative.
- See that the communication plan is complete and that potential omissions and errors have been identified and corrected.
- Develop specific action plans to address barriers to each communication medium.
- Ensure that components of the communication process (as detailed in the other Communication Barriers) that historically have been hurdles for the organization have been addressed.

The information can be placed in a matrix (as shown in Table 2) with critical areas highlighted that provides the communications team with a visual representation of its potential barriers.

Share the plan with the initiative's sponsors to gain support. This is important because the sponsors are frequently required to carry much of the communications load. They often make the presentations, author and sign the memos, and demonstrate desired behavior.

WHO? IN WHAT MANNER?

Communications planning needs to be driven by a formal communications team. Typically included in such a team are individuals

TABLE 2

Action Planning Matrix to Address Communication Barriers

Barrier	What Does It Look Like When Done Right?	Which Population (s) Was Affected?	Why Was It a Problem Before? How Was It Addressed?	How Can We Make It Work? Who Must Do What, by When?

from work units responsible for the *people issues* related to initiatives. It is helpful for them to see themselves as change agents who drive change through communication.

The initiative implementation team should designate specific individuals within their team or include dedicated outside resources to:

- Be responsible for the assessment process.
- Plan the communications.
- Develop the actual communications media.

A NOTE OF CAUTION: It is dangerous to include only those who are focused on companywide communication—they may not understand the intent, context, content, and application of the initiative nor be familiar with nuances of specifically targeted employee groups.

Lack of *Open* Communication

	Preimplementation	During Implementation
Troubleshooting		
Preventative Action		✓

Self-Assessment Questions

1. Has your group agreed on a definition of open communication—one that is written and commonly shared throughout the organization?
2. Do individuals within the organization practice open communication rather than limiting and guarding information because of its power?
3. Do people in your organization regularly embrace rather than shoot the messengers when they present negative or unpopular viewpoints and information?

If You Answered No, Beware! Time and energy will be lost to hidden agendas and convoluted communications.

WHAT NEEDS TO BE DONE?

Open communication requires that everyone in the organization is able to readily obtain all the information they require to proactively participate in the initiative. In order for the organization to achieve a climate for open communication, it must:

- Establish a common definition. If one half of your constituency thinks open communication means *all information is available to everyone* while the other half considers open to mean *give people access to only the specific information they need to do their job,* you will not have an open environment. Once the definition is developed, it needs to be agreed to by key players and clearly and broadly communicated throughout the organization.
- Populate power positions with individuals who do not use their power to withhold information. Sharing information, especially if it was not shared before, constitutes a form of relinquishing power. People need to recognize that other benefits (more important than information power) are gained when information is shared freely (e.g., people have enough information to make the initiative successful).
- Provide comprehensive feedback. Examples of inappropriate feedback commonly practiced are as follows: 1) In some organizations it is acceptable to give the good news but not the bad (people in these organizations talk about shooting the messengers). 2) In others, the group prides itself on being effective critics—they identify what is wrong and let you know (people in these organizations feel that everyone should be self-motivated enough to acquire important information on their own and not need to have it delivered to them). Balanced feedback is required that helps individuals develop trust and respect for both sender and receiver.
- Allow greater access to upper level management. This implies the ability to go at least one level above your manager.
- Listen to others with understanding.
- Establish a senior management team that actively and visibly elicits information from the entire workforce.

WHY? WHAT ARE THE BENEFITS?

A critical issue that is frequently raised when initiatives are dissected is that the organization lacks "boundaryless" communication. People are restricted by the walls that get erected between work and business units. To counter this, individuals must learn to be comfortable with cross-functional communication. If the roadblocks to open communication are allowed to persist, the communication process will be hampered and the initiative will falter.

Open communication will enhance the organization's responsiveness and flexibility—critical elements in today's global, information-driven environment. Openness is a key component of today's effective, flat organizational models. The open climate minimizes the desire to retain information as a source of power. Instead, value is placed on how openly and quickly information can be shared, and "power" is with those who have the skill to facilitate this flow.

Open, two-way communication is a tool to enhance the outcome of the initiative. If the organization does not take time early in the process to establish this climate, it will spend excessive time later to fix the problems of a closed environment. When it is safe to share ideas, employees become a rich resource of initiative and organizational improvement ideas. Respect, trust, and credibility increase when information is shared and correlated with improved performance.

HOW? A RECIPE FOR ACTION

The key is to develop a shared, common definition of open communication that everyone agrees to and supports. The tone must be set throughout the entire organization; everyone must adopt the behavior. One technique to achieve this norm is to treat the definition as a "contract" that is printed and signed by all. It can be posted publicly, at each corporate site, in a place where everyone can see and celebrate it.

> A NOTE OF CAUTION: A danger with this technique is that people who have not bought in to the definition will sign it anyway because of its visibility and peer pressure.

Managers should be accountable for establishing the climate of openness within their own areas. Information must flow down, up, and across the organization. Each communicator is responsible for sharing with one level down, above, and across from his or her own. Those who demonstrate this openness should be rewarded in a public manner.

Another measure of an open-communication climate is the ease with which people are able to interact between various levels. Some activities which are commonly present in open environments include:

- Opportunity for "huddling." This lets individuals talk business freely and informally.
- Encouragement of "boundaryless" communication. This facilitates the flow of new ideas across business units.
- Structured discussion sessions that mix employee levels or are planned so that upper managers can talk to employees with or without immediate managers present.
- Use of e-mail, fax, electronic bulletin boards, and open telephone lines to key executives. This allows individuals to ask (by name or anonymously) questions and get direct responses from those with the information.

An evaluation process needs to be established to determine the organization's degree of openness. Criteria that should be included in the evaluation process are shown in Table 1; add items as appropriate.

The gaps between current and required levels of openness identify areas that the team needs to plan for and the organization needs to work at developing.

WHO? IN WHAT MANNER?

Senior managers are responsible for setting an open tone, and everyone in the organization is responsible for insuring that open communication exists.

The process of creating the communication plan to achieve openness is generally the responsibility of the initiative's design team, supported by communications experts. This team will suggest

TABLE 1

Assessment Criteria for an Open Climate

Evaluation Criteria	Degree of Openness—To Be Defined by the Team	
	Current Degree	Degree Required for Successful Implementation
1. Degree of comfort with expressing your opinion.		
2. Ability to focus on the other person's perspective.		
3. Skill in leading face-to-face communication.		
4. Facilitation skill—i.e., insuring that everyone has the opportunity to join in the discussion.		
5. Skill in asking and answering open and closed questions about the initiative.		
6. Ability to share feelings in a rational, logical manner.		
7. Degree that reaction to messages lack biased judgments and refrain from putting others on guard.		
8. Skill in listening, showing empathy.		
9. Create a feeling of equality and unconditional willingness to share.		

various methods for achieving openness. Managers must be accountable for implementation within their area of authority.

The use of devices such as open contracts reinforces the involvement of everyone in the process. Beyond management's accountability, each workgroup must be responsible for incorporating openness into its daily operations.

Inability to Harness the Informal Communication Channels

	Preimplementation	During Implementation
Troubleshooting	✔	
Preventative Action		

Self-Assessment Questions

1. Does the company control/influence the medium that employees consider to be their "best" source of information?
2. Do managers and employees tap into the same communication systems?
3. Are the same messages being communicated through the formal and informal lines of communication?

If You Answered No, Beware! Management is denied access to vital communication links.

WHAT NEEDS TO BE DONE?

The purpose of a strategic communication plan is to present a total picture of how information flows within the organization. This includes recognizing and charting the informal channels. Leaders of the initiative's communication efforts must be able to tap into the various informal communication networks that exist within the organization. Examples found in most organizations today include gathering spots within the building (i.e., elevators, hallways, and bathrooms), car or van pools, commuter transportation, smoking areas, golf courses, sports clubs, civic meetings, and other social gathering spots. Personal history, experiences, mystique, and validity of past messages influence what people are willing to listen to and believe in—and often this is the informal rather than formal communication.

Harnessing the process requires recognizing and analyzing informal communication channels and understanding how they work. Influencing informal communication is difficult because of issues of trust and credibility. New methods may be needed to penetrate and maximize influence over these channels.

An assessment of the information shared in both informal and formal channels can reveal patterns and gaps. A plan can be developed to close the gaps in the various channels between what is transmitted and determine the degree of credence it is accorded. The assessment provides those responsible for communication with accurate information to ensure that consistent messages flow and to influence the channels.

WHY? WHAT ARE THE BENEFITS?

Communication is the glue that holds an initiative together. It can be a powerful tool for getting people involved and exciting them about an initiative. Organizations often recognize that various channels exist but forget their power. Formal channels are public and have established access means. Informal channels have unstructured access and are harder to tap into, influence, maximize, or measure. They are much more flexible and powerful.

A complete communication plan identifies and incorporates informal channels. If a clear understanding of the *why* and *what* of the initiative are not conveyed through the formal communication vehicles, people in the organization will make assumptions. If they fill in the blanks through informal, unharnessed channels, they can end up misunderstanding the initiative's purpose. This results in the need to *undo* and *redo* the misconceptions, and repeated (or reworked) messages have proved to be excessively costly and time consuming.

If an organization is trying to influence the informal channels, it must recognize the ramifications of such a attempt. The organization must ask how individuals will view such involvement. Reaction can range from its being considered a form of "espionage" or an underhanded management trick, to total unawareness because it was done so transparently. If the workforce construes involvement to be negative, the initiative will fail. If effective, it can heighten the communication process. When the communication planners are able to penetrate informal communication channels in a constructive way, they can help to clarify the goals, rationale, and purpose of the initiative.

This process of tapping into informal communication is necessary because the formal channels don't always get the message to the audience in a timely and appropriate way. Too often, managers are the keepers of all the facts. They assume that what they choose to impart through the formal vehicles is sufficient. They discount other forms and don't plan around them.

HOW? A RECIPE FOR ACTION

Begin with an assessment of your communication channels to determine:

- What channels are operating, both formal and informal?
- Who participates in the various channels, both as listeners and as contributors?
- Who controls each of the channels? This is sometimes difficult to determine for informal channels; however, finding out can be key to disseminating accurate information within the organization.

- How effective is each channel? Establish some method to measure the effectiveness.

The gathered information is the basis for developing a strategy to include the informal networks as acceptable delivery systems for the initiative's messages.

The process includes carefully assessing all aspects of communication—participants as well as medium. The checklist in Table 1 includes elements that you might consider in this evaluation process.

The communication team can use the checklist as a planning tool. Respond to each item, analyze the factors to identify patterns, and determine what additional research should be conducted. The summarized information is the basis for the communication action plan.

WHO? IN WHAT MANNER?

A broad range of people must be involved in the process of communicating information about the initiative. This is especially important if an organization is to effectively tap into informal networks. A communication team serves as the clearinghouse, insuring that all channels relay the same message. The team is responsible for the formal communication plan; in addition, they need to be aware of the informal channels and be prepared to influence them. To achieve this, the team must include individuals who have a great deal of credibility within the organization. Position does not determine credibility.

Communicators from all levels of the organization need to be involved to create a balance. Be sure to include:

- High-level people who will give the initiative clout and priority.
- Key influencers—those who are positioned to share messages because of their networks.
- Communication experts—people who are knowledgeable about the "how's" of communication and committed to sharing messages consistent with the focus of the initiative.

TABLE 1

Checklist of Communication Evaluation

Factors Influencing Effective Communication	Are We Clear on the Factor? Y/N	If Yes, Give Examples of the Factor in Operation	If No, What Research/ Action Is Required to Get to Yes
1. Have we identified all of the communication vehicles, both formal and informal, within the organization?			
2. Do we understand the cultures and audiences present in the organization?			
3. Do we know who controls/influences the message going to our audiences?			
4. Are we able to supersede the grapevine as a key source for information about the initiative?			
5. Do we understand the informal channels? Can we use our relationships in these channels as a *hook* to get employees to buy in?			
6. Do we know how people receive their first piece of information on a particular subject?			
7. Does a message about the initiative go out through the informal channels? Is it frequent enough to gain and maintain support?			
8. Are all messages (intended and formal/informal and unintended) that go out consistent with the goals and direction of the initiative?			
9. Is employee opinion shifting toward the initiative because informal channels were tapped?			

Not Measuring the Effectiveness of Internal Communication

	Preimplementation	During Implementation
Troubleshooting		✔
Preventative Action		

Self-Assessment Questions

1. Are you aware of what percentage of your organization reads printed material (i.e., bulletins about the progress and accomplishments of an initiative)?
2. Does your organization have the ability to measure the usage of a specific communication medium?
3. Do you measure employees' degree of understanding of your improvement initiative?

If You Answered No, Beware! Resources are wasted supporting communication channels on which nobody relies.

WHAT NEEDS TO BE DONE?

Successful endeavors disseminate massive amounts of information at various times and in various ways throughout the initiative's lifecycle. An initiative's communication process needs to include feedback and self-corrective mechanisms to assess effectiveness. Data collection and feedback loops need to be installed at appropriate points so that an ongoing evaluation process occurs.

The goal of communication evaluation is to provide actionable data to improve the alignment of messages with the initiative's mission. Elements that must be included in the process to achieve effective communication are:

- Develop concrete measures of effectiveness.
- Create a plan for collecting the observable data.
- Track and analyze employee responses.
- Identify and share key findings.
- Target specific areas for improvement.
- Measure and report on the effectiveness of the communication media.

A comprehensive feedback plan will ensure that information regarding communication media and strategies are evaluated regularly during the initiative's phases. This allows for corrective action to be taken and ensures that the communication serves its purpose of enhancing initiative support.

WHY? WHAT ARE THE BENEFITS?

The purpose of communication is to get the message out to employees—to enhance the efficient transfer of information—in a cost-effective manner. Ineffective strategies and plans can create a communication chain but do not guarantee acceptance of and action upon the words. Measurement is the barometer of success. When measurement is carefully designed and initiated, the data will tell if a specific message was effective; i.e., did those who received the information hear and act upon it as expected? Too often, sponsors omit the evaluation because it is not easy to do for a "soft" skill like communication.

HOW? A RECIPE FOR ACTION

Methods of measurement must be established that focus on the receiver's acceptance of and action toward the message. The goal is to develop measures that describe/reflect observable behaviors. The effectiveness of internal measures can be determined through the systematic use of statistically oriented techniques. Examples include:

- Surveys
- Questionnaires
- Direct observations
- Self-reported data
- Check sheets

Each of these tools assesses employees' perceptions of the communication's effectiveness.

The developers' first task is to clarify the term "effective communication." This will ensure that the development team uses the term in a uniform fashion. Next, the developers concretely outline the *what's* and *why's* of the instrument:

- The purpose of the instrument and its use.
- The outcome, impact, and/or result to be gained from collecting and analyzing the data.
- The utility of data gathered—insuring that the information is actionable.

The model in Table 1 outlines a sequence that might be followed to design a tool to gather workforce perception.

WHO? IN WHAT MANNER?

People involved in the measurement process need two skill sets: design and application. These skills may or may not be found in the same people.

Design skill is necessary to develop an effective measurement tool and interpret the collected information. To design the measurement tool, individuals need an understanding of statistical analysis and survey design. Some organizations have such individuals on

TABLE 1

Tool Development Model

Step 1	Brainstorm a list of statements, factors, and conditions the developers want respondents to evaluate.
Step 2	Prioritize the list, highlighting key statements.
Step 3	Recreate the list displaying the general statements first leading to the more specific statements.
Step 4	Select the appropriate scale for responses—e.g., Likert (5- to 7-point scales), forced choice (even option number to reflect +/-), and both open- and closed-ended items (tell me about the questions versus selecting from the listed options).
Step 5	Pretest the tool three times before using it with the targeted population—refine after each pretest.
Step 6	Determine the appropriate respondent mix—all employees, random selection, targeted group.
Step 7	Administer the tool. Carefully consider the issues of method of administration (in person, group meeting, by mail) and need for anonymity (should respondents be identified or given the option of remaining anonymous?). Direct communication offers opportunity for clarification of statements and signifies that the developers are interested in the feedback.
Step 8	Analyze responses.
Step 9	Determine opportunities for improvement.
Step 10	Communicate and implement recommendations.
Step 11	Loop the process back to reassessing the appropriateness of the instrument items to provide information needed by the developers.

staff in market research, quality assurance, performance engineering, or ISO 9000 areas.

Application skill involves applying the collected data to improve the initiative design (generally the responsibility of the sponsors, communicators, and implementation team). Analysis and communication skills are critical in this role. Selected individuals must have the presence within the organization to ensure accurate and timely feedback to those who participate in the measurement process and those involved in the initiative itself.

24 The Predicament of Making Mistakes

BARRIER

	Preimplementation	During Implementation
Troubleshooting		✔
Preventative Action		

Self-Assessment Questions

1. Does your organization encourage people to discuss issues across organizational boundaries?
2. Does your organization "reward" rather than penalize employees who make mistakes?
3. Are mistakes used to facilitate learning?
4. Is information regarding mistakes collected and shared to prevent similar errors from recurring?

If You Answered No, Beware! Fear of reprisal means that no one offers opposition or takes risks, and the organization continues to perpetuate the same mistakes.

WHAT NEEDS TO BE DONE?

In most organizations, mistakes are a natural phenomenon. The experience gained from these mistakes can be collected and used to help the organization achieve the initiative's goals. If errors become an embarrassment, their occurrence is often suppressed or not recorded in a fashion that others can use—the knowledge is lost. In many cases when it is communicated and documented, the "mistake" later shows up as a "negative comment" in a performance review.

When organizations positively focus their attention on mistakes, improvements can occur. The organization needs to provide time to analyze a mistake and identify the root cause. After the information is collected and recorded, it should be communicated to others who might benefit from it. This method treats mistakes as part of the learning process.

Technology can help to develop an on-line system to track mistakes as they occur; problems can be documented and shared amongst workgroups. This approach allows the organization to quickly solve problems and prevent them from recurring. When the process is perfected, the data should be available to others at the time the mistake occurs.

WHY? WHAT ARE THE BENEFITS?

As companies demand more from an overworked population through initiatives and other critical priorities, the opportunities for error increase. Often problems occur in one part of the organization and are duplicated in others. The information is not shared across work units, and unnecessary repetition and rework results. This impedes the organization and fosters an environment where mistakes are viewed as job threatening.

In too many organizations, a public admission of a mistake is political suicide. The workforce either totally avoids making decisions that might lead to mistakes, or it secretly hides those that are made. The result is an organization in which no one will take risks. This behavior pattern obstructs bold initiatives and loses valuable cross-unit learning. Employees spend more time protecting themselves than fixing or preventing the errors, and the status quo becomes the norm.

Organizations must learn to use errors as a way to expand knowledge; as the cliché has it, they must learn from their mistakes. By evaluating and converting mistakes into knowledge, both the individual and the organization can benefit, and errors are seen as worthwhile. Learning occurs because the error is seen from a different point of view, and this approach signals to employees that making mistakes is safe.

HOW? A RECIPE FOR ACTION

Taking time to admit, bring out, and discuss problems sends a message that the leadership does not consider mistakes wrong or negative. Some techniques that work:

1. *Encourage openness* about mistakes, so that relevant information can be collected. Post mistakes on specified bulletin boards, whether on a wall bulletin board using Post-it™ notes, or through e-mail or electronic bulletin boards. The mistake should be listed as a problem with a proposed solution, as an issue that still needs to be resolved, or as a question. Requests for input to unresolved issues and questions encourage employees to creatively develop possible alternatives. This allows respondents to freely brainstorm problems and solutions without identifying the owner.

A NOTE OF CAUTION: To make this approach more powerful, have influential managers share, in written form, several mistakes they have made. Although a signature is optional, doing so will increase the impact of their sharing.

2. Have managers *discuss key mistakes* they have made. This will pave the way for open discussion and should encourage employees to share their problems.

A NOTE OF CAUTION: The rules for making mistakes must be the same for managers and for individual contributors. Different repercussions leads to distrust of the approach, especially on the part of nonmanagers.

3. *Conduct forums* where critical mistakes are discussed. This can be done with existing workgroups or interested individuals. Managers present key mistakes, and participants brainstorm and explore alternative solutions.

A NOTE OF CAUTION: Ensure that the person(s) who made the mistake is comfortable with sharing it.

4. *Hold review meetings* of the initiative at critical milestones to examine what has occurred. These meetings should include all those who were accountable and who supported the accomplishment of the specific milestone. A facilitator should lead a discussion about what worked, what did not, and how things could have been done differently. The facilitator may want to use the force field analysis technique to identify the helpful and constraining factors. The ideas should be recorded and disseminated.

A NOTE OF CAUTION: A postmortem is the minimal standard for initiative review.

Since the objective is to create conditions for learning and not for hiding mistakes, conclude the open discussions, forums, and review sessions by having participants discuss the following:

- What was learned by discussing the mistake?
- How can this error be applied to a specific job or workgroup?
- What lessons can be carried forth to future initiatives; who will keep the information and take responsibility for sharing it?
- How can the information be disseminated to other work groups?

Be sure to positively recognize the contribution of the person who made the mistake—and keep in mind that this can be done humorously.

WHO? IN WHAT MANNER?

The review meetings need to be led by someone who can promote discussion of sensitive issues. The meeting leader is responsible for making it safe for varying points of view to be aired while protecting the respect and dignity of the parties involved. The leader cannot let participants talk around issues. He or she must keep discussions open, minimize defensiveness, keep people focused on the right issues, and drive the meeting toward action.

An experienced facilitator may be needed to assist managers in leading the open discussions, forums, and reviews. The facilitator can help managers ask questions that challenge the "sacred cows" and encourage alternative ways of thinking. If your organization does not have qualified facilitators, it is a worthwhile investment to hire a consultant to develop these skills in your leader ranks. The consultant will need to provide feedback and make suggestions on how managers can improve their performance for future meetings.

READING 24–1

An automobile dealership found an effective technique was to look openly at their own inadequate experience with customers. The data was gathered from observation and complaints. They asked themselves if they were the customer would they feel satisfied or dissatisfied with the encounter. Discussions were held weekly to look for ways to improve aspects of their service.

HUMAN FACTOR

The Heart of the Initiative

	Preimplementation	During Implementation
Troubleshooting	27. Not developing initiative cheerleaders. 30. Forgetting key parties. 35. Not confronting the resistance to the initiative.	28. Changes midstream in executive leadership. 36. No time for the initiative. 37. Avoiding performance management issues.
Preventative Action	26. Not developing the initiative's sponsors. 31. Not minimizing human foibles. 32. Relationship of staff competency to initiative success. 34. Not fostering creative, visionary thinking.	25. Initiative isn't a reality to top management. 29. Lack of competent, assertive management. 33. Not embracing middle management.

Organizations must recognize that their most valuable asset is their workforce. Indeed, organizations are only as effective as the individuals who populate them. Capable people are a scarce resource, and as organizations adopt initiatives the human factor becomes a greater barrier. Therefore, organizations must enhance the capacity for individual and organizational performance as they implement initiatives.

A long-term, collaborative plan must be devised that focuses on increasing performance levels of human capital. Two broad categories that must be considered when dealing with the human factor are:

1. *Get the right audiences involved.* Any initiative will involve many people and groups. Care must be taken to include the right people from all ranks and arenas and provide them with support to ensure maximum contribution.

2. *Deal with people from a holistic view.* Involve employees as full partners by:

- Identifying the new skills and competencies required by the initiative—for both managers and nonmanagers.
- Assessing these skills against the workforce's current capabilities.
- Developing and nurturing the workforce to understand the importance of altering behaviors.
- Understanding each individual's and workgroup's capacity for accepting change.
- Ensuring that change occurs and that it is everyone's responsibility.

People attempt to fit their behavior to the situation. Initiative leaders are required to create an environment where continuous learning and creative potential can flourish. The organization needs employees who desire to attain knowledge and are flexible, compassionate, and responsive. Leaders must prevent the reinforcement of patterns and personalities that do not adopt the new expectations. Barriers that inhibit the growth of human potential as part of initiative implementation include:

- Not "managing" all levels of management involvement.

- Not identifying or clarifying responsibilities of sponsors and cheerleaders.
- Ignoring key stakeholders.
- Neglecting the creative component of the initiative.
- Not creating or expressing performance expectations.

Overcoming these barriers increases the ownership for the initiative while minimizing the possibility of a counterculture developing.

Initiative Isn't a Reality to Top Management

	Preimplementation	During Implementation
Troubleshooting		
Preventative Action		✓

Self-Assessment Questions

1. Is senior management engaged in the initiative?
2. Does executive management share common expectations for the initiative?
3. Does senior management adopt the new rules to demonstrate support for the endeavor?

If You Answered No, Beware! No one will take the initiative seriously because commitment does not come from the top.

WHAT NEEDS TO BE DONE?

Most endeavors fall short of their intended results because of a lack of executive engagement. Initiatives are effective when senior managers direct employee participation and commitment toward attaining initiative goals and performing effectively using the revised rules and behaviors. Senior managers must provide enough information so that the workforce can see the need for behavior changes. They need to be excited and sincere about the initiative and paint a clear, concrete picture of how the organization will progress to the new state.

Top management needs to stay connected with the initiative by evaluating the impact the revised rules have on the organization. Executive management must demonstrate commitment by investing time, enthusiasm, and attention, and adopting the behaviors that will make the endeavor succeed.

WHY? WHAT ARE THE BENEFITS?

The fundamental reason to begin an initiative is to change the behavior of the organization. Initiatives are deployed in organizations through senior management, yet senior managers, though often aware of the potential results of the initiative, minimize their involvement after initializing the endeavor. Whether through a lack of guidance or education, they make an inadequate effort, continue to function as before, and add the endeavor to a list of overburdened priorities.

Senior managers cannot authorize others to lead the effort. Without personal engagement, there is great risk that the endeavor will fail. Employees want to hear directly from the executive leaders, not from intermediaries who act as the bosses' mouthpiece. Nonparticipation conveys aloofness, which encourages employees to question top management's commitment. When the initiative is actively guided by senior management, employees will embrace it.

HOW? A RECIPE FOR ACTION

Although there are no simple steps to ensure that senior management is totally committed to an initiative, senior managers can demonstrate commitment by:

- Educating themselves by talking to other executives and attending conferences where other senior executives share initiative-related experiences. Top management may conduct visits to other companies to see how they have implemented the initiative. They need to evaluate the information presented, not merely repeat or accept for their company what other leaders have said or done.

- Ensuring that the effort will significantly improve organization performance before involving others; i.e., assuring that it has applicability. They should then evaluate how it might be integrated into the mission, strategies, and goals of the company.

- Creating a shared vision, strategies, and procedures. It is critical that they *enthusiastically* share the key strategies of the initiative and state how the company will achieve its goals. This sets the tone that they are leading the effort.

- Authorizing and actively supporting a team of people who have respect, skill, and knowledge of the business and of the initiative to ensure that plans are developed and clearly stated in ways that relate to jobs and functions.

- Staying attuned and ensuring that the initiative stays on track. During implementation, top managers should require the analysis of lessons learned to improve the process by adapting new approaches and using different techniques.

- Engaging in a structured discussion with each other to share issues and address obstacles. A facilitator should conduct the session and promote dialogue on how to keep or get the initiative on track. The discussions should produce agreement among these managers and generate strategies for improvement.

WHO? IN WHAT MANNER?

The catalyst is an energized executive management group who understand and are committed to the initiative. This is best facilitated through the use of a consultant who is expert in the initiative and in dealing with senior managers. Criteria used to evaluate the appropriateness of the consultant include:

- An expert on the issues driving the initiative.
- Viewed as credible by executive management.
- Unafraid to challenge traditional thinking and raise critical issues.
- Positioned to drive senior managers to action and influence the real decision makers.

READING 25–1

The CEO of a small entrepreneurial firm terminated a direct report. The deciding factor for the termination was the individual's lack of passion and active support for the initiative, which the CEO was driving.

Not Developing the Initiative's Sponsors

	Preimplementation	During Implementation
Troubleshooting		
Preventative Action	✔	

Self-Assessment Questions

1. Have you identified sponsors for each stage of the initiative?
2. Through careful selection, are you able to minimize the drop-off/drop-out rate among those you recruit as initiative sponsors?
3. Do you have a structured plan in place to provide ongoing support for people who sponsor your improvement initiatives?

If You Answered No, Beware! Ineffective sponsors can't manage the change, move the organization forward, or achieve results.

WHAT NEEDS TO BE DONE?

Sponsors are critical to the success of any improvement initiative. Sponsors must be able to drive the initiative and guide decision making. Strategic planning for the initiative requires determining the profile of roles, accountabilities, authority levels, skills, and networks needed for each sponsor(s). People who first introduce the initiative into the organization must understand these factors and be prepared to recruit appropriately.

In addition to selecting the right people to sponsor the initiative, equal attention must be paid to developing and nurturing these individuals. The initiative planners must be prepared to:

- Clearly define roles and responsibilities.
- Determine decision-making and authority levels.
- Coach the sponsors.
- Provide support.
- Provide networks.
- Plan ahead for future needs.

The most obvious sponsor-candidates may possess clout and business knowledge but fail to see the value of the endeavor to the organization. Sponsors will contribute to the fullest of their capabilities only if they share the beliefs and values of the initiative.

WHY? WHAT ARE THE BENEFITS?

The success of an improvement initiative is generally measured over the long term—was there a sustained change in productivity, behavior, or some other measure? Successful long-term initiatives require ongoing support. This will not occur unless the stages are clearly delineated: i.e., what is needed, why, and who can best provide the necessary clout and leadership? The skills that can generate initial enthusiasm and create the direction for a new initiative are not necessarily the same ones that are required in the maintenance phase. Advantages of recruiting according to stage include:

- Having the right people provide guidance and direction for the initiative at the appropriate time in its lifecycle.

- With a well-orchestrated initiative, people within the organization understand the stages and appreciate the changes in sponsorship.
- Recognition that different technical skills will be required to sustain the initiative gives greater credence to the effort and to the selection of sponsors to match needs. Unless this is publicly shared, however, people will associate sponsorship changes with loss of initiative value.
- People are positive about participation because their skills complement the phase; they are in sync.

HOW? A RECIPE FOR ACTION

It is the responsibility of those initiating the endeavor to think through the requirements for the sponsors. The matrix in Table 1 provides a guide for the types of questions that need to be answered before sponsors are recruited. After the kinds of support and skills are identified, the next step is to clarify what is expected of them and what needs to be done "behind-the-scenes" to make their job of sponsorship easier.

> If the sponsor and the contribution needed at a given stage don't match, the individual feels frustrated, is reluctant to put time into the initiative, and projects a less than positive attitude. This is picked up on by those observing the sponsor, and a bad attitude begins to spread throughout the organization.

WHO? IN WHAT MANNER?

The senior person or team driving the initiative either identifies sponsors directly or is responsible for selecting the team that will take responsibility for the process. People who would be appropriate for such an assignment include:

- Individuals who know the organization and its human resources well.

TABLE 1

Clarification of Sponsorship Requirements and Support

Initiative Stage— What Is Happening? What Skills Does the Sponsor Need?	What Kind of Support Is Needed to Ensure Sponsor's Success?	What Time and Energy Commitment Is Needed?	Who Could Best Provide the Support?

- Consultants/experts who are familiar with the generic initiative and are able to spell out the types of sponsorship and associated skills that are usually required.
- People who have the authority to recruit the identified sponsors.

This team needs to identify requirements up front and assess how well the recruits are meeting the needs of the initiative. Were the appropriate people selected? Were the requirements spelled out correctly? Have changes occurred in initiative design that require a different skill set?

Not Developing Initiative Cheerleaders

	Preimplementation	During Implementation
Troubleshooting	✓	
Preventative Action		

Self-Assessment Questions

1. Has the organization identified key individuals who can promote the initiative?
2. Are individuals positioned in the organization to publicly celebrate success?
3. Does the organization have energetic people who willingly "cheer" employees who embrace the new philosophy?

If You Answered No, Beware! No one is positioned to excite employees toward action or to maintain momentum.

WHAT NEEDS TO BE DONE?

To encourage acceptance of the initiative, the organization needs to identify "key" individuals who can act as cheerleaders for the effort. These individuals need to publicly proclaim and cheer the endeavor and keep it at the forefront of everyone's minds. They exert their zeal to create or sustain the motivation of the workgroups. Cheerleaders also can advertise successes and inform the workforce when problems are resolved. These people are not necessarily the champions or the sponsors; they must be positioned so as to exert a degree of power, but their contribution is based on their ability to generate enthusiastic support for the initiative.

The cheerleader's role is to inspire change by advocating urgency and need for change. They embody the initiative; they are role models, creating the environment and vitality needed for the initiative to be adopted. Their supportive actions involve listening, creating excitement, encouraging, and helping employees perform the necessary activities of the endeavor.

WHY? WHAT ARE THE BENEFITS?

Success is generally measured over the initiative's duration. After the endeavor has been in existence for a while it becomes more difficult to sustain enthusiasm. Although each circumstance is distinct, most initiatives require cheerleaders who can vivaciously support the effort.

Cheerleaders help to formulate the workforce's opinion about the initiative and reconfirm the organization's commitment to the endeavor. Contact with cheerleaders has positive effects—it proves the company is "walking the talk" and motivates employees to continue embracing the new behaviors. They add value by involving those who are "watching from the fence" and minimizing the wait-and-see attitudes.

HOW? A RECIPE FOR ACTION

Well-selected and positioned cheerleaders reduce opposition and help the organization "win" by instituting the initiative as a permanent way of doing business. Senior managers need to recruit individuals to serve as devoted ambassadors demonstrating and reinforcing the new patterns the company wants to see. These individuals take action and foster an environment in which it is safe for employees to try the new initiative behaviors.

It is important that the organization chooses individuals who have an accurate vision of what needs to be achieved as well as the energy, enthusiasm, credibility, and respect to make a difference. During the various stages of implementation this role may be shared by several people. Table 1 will help you identify the individuals and the unique talents they need to be effective.

WHO? IN WHAT MANNER?

The cheerleaders should be energetic, respected individuals who are able to publicly demonstrate and communicate their commitment. Select people who are willing to demonstrate advocacy by:

- Regularly visiting workgroups to reinforce actions.
- Being knowledgeable about the initiative.
- Demonstrating an ability to provide guidance and motivation to workgroups.
- Having a comprehensive outlook of the business.
- Being strong individuals who will not fold under the pressure of opponents of the initiative.

TABLE 1

Identification of Cheerleaders

		Talents Required		
Initiative Stage— What Is Happening?	What Kind of Cheerleading Is Needed?	What Time and Energy Commitment Is Necessary?	Who Could Best Provide the Needed Support?	Have They Filled a Familiar Role? What Were the Outcomes?

Changes Midstream in Executive Leadership

	Preimplementation	During Implementation
Troubleshooting		✓
Preventative Action		

Self-Assessment Questions

1. Are you aware of the business philosophy of the new leader?
2. Have you identified personal associates whom you can contact to gain information about the new CEO?
3. Has the initiative team or sponsor established channels of communication with the new CEO to explore his or her perceptions, experiences, views regarding the endeavor?

If You Answered No, Beware! Initiative flounders because new CEO has a different agenda.

WHAT NEEDS TO BE DONE?

Changes in executive leadership can have a major impact on initiatives. If the new CEO (that is, the most senior-level individual over the entire organizational body implementing the initiative) has a different frame of reference, or does not understand or endorse it, the effort will experience a major delay or cancellation.

The relationship between the CEO and sponsors must be managed so that the initiative has the best chance of success. Initially, sponsors need to get a reading on how the new CEO sees, feels about, and has dealt with similar initiatives in the past. All early efforts must be focused on gaining insights on the individual and determining modifications or actions needed to foster the initiative under the new regime. A key is to proactively gather information and not waste energy getting caught up in the anxiety of the "change of command." Public and personal observations can be gathered by:

- Referencing public information—looking at the track record and philosophy of the CEO in previous organizations or positions.
- Subtly feeling out how the CEO stands by listening closely to his or her remarks at companywide meetings, one-on-ones, and so on.
- Using informal networks of peers and consultants to discover how other organizations handled similar situations or how this new CEO reacted.

By deciphering the information, the sponsors may uncover a creative approach on how to win the CEO's support for the endeavor. The goal is to present the initiative in a way that generates buy-in and commitment from the new leader. However, the investigation may indicate that the initiative needs to be severely modified or scrapped.

WHY? WHAT ARE THE BENEFITS?

A critical success factor for any initiative is the support of the CEO. Having a leadership change in midstream makes this support tenuous. The investigation that the initiative sponsors orchestrate must establish the degree of support they can expect from the new officer. Low levels of support spell difficulty for the initiative; high levels suggest that the initiative can continue, with some modifications to accommodate the new CEO's interests. However, this determination cannot be made if the sponsors don't know this individual's views.

HOW? A RECIPE FOR ACTION

Methods for gaining insight about the new CEO include:

- Identify the CEO's track record/philosophy. Be specific. Learn about the new CEO's business principles, past organizational affiliations, college and graduate school philosophies, business approaches, personal value system, personal operational style, and whether he or she has any unwritten rules that must be obeyed.
- Determine how the effort fits in with the CEO's perspective. Review the information in relationship to the initiative to determine similarities and differences. Weigh their potential impact on the endeavor.
- Identify others who had to resolve this problem. Understand how they were able to positively influence the new CEO to engage in the endeavor. Don't limit your search only to contacts who had success. Focus on the lessons learned from those who failed. What would they do differently?
- Identify others who were able to influence the CEO in the past. Uncover through personal networks individuals who have influenced the thoughts of the new leader.
- Assess what was learned. Evaluate the information obtained; summarize and ascertain how the information can help the initiative. Identify strategies and actions that can be implemented.

Once the information is analyzed, sponsors will need to decide how best to encourage the CEO's engagement. They will need to focus on a business rationale that positions the endeavor as a tool to leverage the organization's performance.

A NOTE OF CAUTION: If it does not appear that the initiative will have the support of the new CEO, the sponsoring team must establish a plan for positively sharing the changed direction with the organization at large. It can be difficult to have touted an initiative that is now "dead" because of the new business philosophy of one person. It is, however, important to be open with employees about what is transpiring. This will impact support for future initiatives under the new CEO.

WHO? IN WHAT MANNER?

The initiative leaders and sponsors are responsible for managing the process of actively involving the new CEO. They need to possess excellent negotiation, networking, diplomacy, and analytical and communication skills.

READING 28-1

The new head of a government agency verbally stated and gave subtle messages that she was not enamored with the existing initiative. Subordinates, who wanted to make a good impression, decided that it was best to end the initiative. Six months later it was resurrected as her own, new idea.

Lack of Competent, Assertive Management

	Preimplementation	During Implementation
Troubleshooting		
Preventative Action		✔

Self-Assessment Questions

1. In your organization, being a manager isn't synonymous with being "taken care of"—i.e., may be moved but not eliminated?
2. Have managerial skills required in the new organization been openly shared with managers and nonmanagers alike?
3. Can the initiative's implementors separate business decisions from personal relationships to ensure that the appropriate human capital is selected for the new managerial jobs?
4. Have managerial ranks changed in conjunction with initiative implementation?

If You Answered No, Beware! The "best" people for the new managerial jobs may be overlooked in favor of those who have proven themselves in the past.

WHAT NEEDS TO BE DONE?

New managerial talent is required to drive the initiative. Those who are introducing the initiative into the organization need to:

- Clearly define what kinds of "new" leadership and managerial skills will be needed to guide the process.
- Require that managers be responsible for the work and development of their employees.
- Assess managerial skills and competencies of the current management team.

The goal of skill assessment is to ensure that the initiative's leaders and managers are competent and assertive. (It is assumed that they have bought into the initiative and will support it wholeheartedly.) The assessment and planning processes must be analytical. Who does and does not have the skills to work effectively in the new environment? Deciding who will participate cannot become a "popularity contest" whereby decision makers try to take care of people who were liked and/or successful in the old environment.

Dealing with selection at the individual manager level can be extremely difficult and uncomfortable. Those who will have to make the hard decisions need to assess their own capability to ensure that they do not demonstrate weak performance management and coaching skills.

WHY? WHAT ARE THE BENEFITS?

In today's rapidly changing business climate, businesses must respond by developing a management team that has the skills, growth potential, and responsibility to obtain the highest levels of performance from all contributors. An organization cannot assume that managers and leaders who were competent in the old environment will succeed in the new one. The organization needs to invest in new leaders who can make the initiative work. Being willing to make significant changes in leadership to match initiative standards makes a strong statement about the organization's commitment to the endeavor. One key to making this happen is to rely upon managers and leaders who have the right skill sets, both technical and behavioral.

The organization needs to articulate and enforce the new leadership requirements and spend less effort on long-term managers who may be loyal but who cannot make the transition. This is a harsh statement, yet the changing workplace suggests that the model of the future will rely upon "portfolio-based" employees (managers and leaders included). Employees will be called upon based on the needs of the job and will be employed as long as they add value to the organization.

Many organizations have had the experience of moving command-and-control managers into a team-based environment. Training and coaching are required to help these individuals make the transition; however, even with support a percentage will be unable to operate effectively in the changed environment. If left in place and not held accountable or monitored, they continue with old behaviors, demoralize their staff, and act as impediments to the "new" system.

HOW? A RECIPE FOR ACTION

The person driving the initiative needs to begin the process by honestly assessing his or her own willingness to take action. Some self-assessment questions are listed in Table 1.

The leader of the initiative will need to carefully identify the competencies, skills, and behaviors needed by management to support the initiative. Each current manager and leader (who needs the personality and knowledge to influence the organization) must be assessed to determine the ratio of new skills needed to skills currently possessed. Include some of the organization's high-potential staff in the evaluation process—people who may be seen as future leaders based on the *new* needs. A sample matrix is shown in Table 2.

Once you have identified the best candidates for leadership and management within the new environment, you can begin to develop plans to ensure that they are ready for their role. You need to invest in training and support systems to prepare and mentor these new leaders. Training is more critical for those who are a match, so that they can achieve their highest levels of performance; this may require outside resources.

TABLE 1

Leader Potential for the New Environment

Assessment Questions	Your Response	Impact This Will Have on Your Ability to Take Action?
1. How willing are you to deal with confrontational issues?		
2. Have you dealt effectively in the past with performance issues?		
3. Do you have support within your organization—from your boss, mentor/coach, consultant, and HR department—to help you deal with any difficult issues?		
4. How willing are you to adopt the new behaviors?		
5. Are you willing to allow teamwork to flourish within your workgroup?		
6. Do you value change over power—status quo thinking?		
7. Are you more comfortable with variability than with consistency?		
8. Can you develop strengths and capabilities to do the required work?		
9. Do you frequently provide feedback to employees about their performance?		
10. Can you navigate a course for employees and influence them to accept it and effectively move ahead?		

A NOTE OF CAUTION: Many training and external resources claim to develop the requisite skills but prove to be ineffectual. They provide immediate results but don't effect long-term change.

You will need to assess whether training can help those who do not match to develop the required performance. If training might make a difference, you will need to determine if the same or different training methods are needed as those used with high-potential staff. For those who will not match, look for other options. This

TABLE 2

Managerial Assessment Matrix

Competency, Skill, Behavior—A Description of What Is Needed	Managers Who Possess the Traits— Person and Degree of Match	Leaders Who Possess the Traits— Person and Degree of Match	High-Potential Managers Who Might Meet the Requirements— Person and Degree of Match	Best Match(es)

process can be quite lengthy. Be sure to handle the assessment and positioning of leadership before you actually begin to implement the initiative. Parallel processes of people development and the design of the initiative's implementation plan are effective as long as they stay in sync.

A NOTE OF CAUTION: Take steps to ensure that your parallel process doesn't take on a life of its own and minimize leadership's ability to make decisions or its authority to deal with performance issues that may arise during the development process.

WHO? IN WHAT MANNER?

The process of identifying required skills for the "new" managerial jobs needs to be done by someone familiar with both the initiative's requirements and generic skill definition. In most cases this is best done by a consultant (internal or external) who has been involved previously with the design and implementation of the particular managerial tool. The assessment of current proficiencies within the managerial and leadership ranks can be done by the managers who currently evaluate the talent pool or by human resource specialists who are familiar with both employees and required skills.

The senior person responsible for implementing the initiative needs to take an active role in making the actual placement decisions. This person may make the decisions alone or with a core management team that has knowledge of the initiative, its staffing requirements, and is familiar with current managers and leaders. Whenever staffing decisions are addressed, the human resources department generally participates in an advisory capacity.

Forgetting Key Parties

	Preimplementation	During Implementation
Troubleshooting	✔	
Preventative Action		

Self-Assessment Questions

1. Do you take the time to clearly identify your top customers and initiative stakeholders?
2. Is there an expectation that all key parties will be included in the process of any initiative?
3. Do you have procedures in place to decide the appropriateness of including customers and other key parties in any initiative?
4. Do you have methods for collecting data from key parties who will not directly be involved in the initiative design process?

If You Answered No, Beware! Initiative design will be incomplete and critical aspects omitted due to lack of comprehensive input.

WHAT NEEDS TO BE DONE?

To be successful, an initiative must adopt a 360° perspective, reflecting the views, concerns, and potential contributions of all affected parties. The initiative's implementation process needs to include a systematic method to identify and include key parties, such as managers, customers (internal as well as external), and members of other work units who interact with the unit undergoing change.

No improvement initiative can assume a totally internal focus and succeed. Those designing the initiative need to be held accountable for insuring that the appropriate outside parties participate. A concerted effort must be made during the initial design stages of an initiative to determine who has an interest in the outcome of the initiative and who might be a valuable resource for information about the endeavor. Those designing the initiative may have difficulty recognizing outsiders who can contribute to its success. The design team can create the initial list, but an external reality check is vital.

WHY? WHAT ARE THE BENEFITS?

Taking a 360° approach to participant selection helps to overcome the parochial view that many units adopt when they undertake an initiative. A 360° perspective assists organizational integration of the endeavor by invoking vital network links. Using this approach the organization is better able to include a "horizontal" mix, provide a more global perspective, and ensure that all critical stakeholders participate. When this broader approach is taken, it is more likely that the initiative will result in improved business operations and increased competitiveness. Involving people and leaders from the impacted functions and processes helps to minimize resistance.

An issue that often surfaces with internally focused initiatives is that the company's internal customers/stakeholders are forgotten. Initiative planners often focus on the external customer and the immediate participants of the process being changed but don't think to ask, "Who else in the organization will be affected by the initiative?" This results in tunnel vision and leads to the neglect of those outside the immediate work unit who may directly or indirectly be impacted and/or pay the cost of the implementation.

HOW ? A RECIPE FOR ACTION

An early step in the design process is to complete a list of all potentially impacted parties, as shown in Table 1.

Impacted parties can be identified through:

- A brainstorming session in which the team thinks of all potential groups.
- Interviewing the authors of official documents to see if they should be included on the team.
- A role-playing session in which the team assumes the role of the initiative moving through its lifecycle, mapping out the involved parties and functions that will be affected.
- Direct observation of the organization to uncover obscure individuals who will be indirectly impacted.
- The development of a quality check that requires the group to periodically ask: "Is there someone else we should be checking with about this initiative?"
- The use of an outside resource to provide a reality check of the list the team generated.

Inclusion of these individuals or groups should optimize their knowledge of the initiative and its environment. Involving them requires a conscious check-off, a mindset that says, "People I must remember as part of this initiative are . . . "

In some organizations the concept of customer and stakeholder is so ingrained that these groups are automatically cultivated. In

TABLE 1

Identifying Impacted Parties

Impacted Parties	Role That They Might Be Recruited to Play	How Severely Will They Be Impacted by the Initiative? (Directly/Indirectly)		
		High	Medium	Low

organizations where this is not the case, some techniques that can be instituted include:

- Having an "advocate" position within each unit. It is the job of this person to make sure that the customer, end user, and other stakeholders are always kept in mind and included.
- Assigning a coach to each team member. It is the responsibility of the coach to guide, provide a broader perspective, reveal impacted parties, and act as a sounding board. It is the responsibility of the team member to actively seek input from this individual, to report back on activities that can be passed throughout the organization, and to "learn" from the association.
- Preparing a checklist to which all initiative planners must refer to ensure that key elements, such as inclusion of the critical stakeholders, are included. The checklist is a requirement of the endeavor's design and implementation phases.
- Developing an awareness or marketing plan that focuses team members on critical players and impacted parties; it becomes everyone's job to identify and watch out for these groups.
- Holding regular focus groups with customers and stakeholders. This allows these individuals to act as their own advocates, query design team members about what is going on, voice their desire to get involved in initiatives when they deem it necessary, and provide input as to what must be included in the endeavor.
- A question such as, "Did we include the right parities?" as part of the postmortem to prevent future omissions.

WHO? IN WHAT MANNER?

Depending upon the size of the initiative it may make sense to have a specialized recruitment team. Their job is to ensure that the right people and groups are included. For smaller initiatives, this task can be done by the team leader. The individual selected to do this job should:

- Be a highly regarded, accomplished project manager and an excellent communicator able to successfully recruit participants.
- Be a futuristic thinker with strong ties to the business units who possesses comprehensive business experience.
- Have a clear vision of what needs to be achieved.
- Possesses the talent to carefully scan the organization to differentiate committed individuals who have no hidden agendas from nonreceptive parties who obstruct the implementation of the initiative.
- Be able to distinguish internal and external factors and determine forces that will need to be dealt with to achieve the involvement of all stakeholders.
- Understand and be committed to the goals of the initiative.
- Be able to think across organizational boundaries and operate effectively in a horizontal organization.
- Demonstrate a willingness to actively participate—be devoted, vivacious, eager, and valued across the organization.
- Have an endorsement from the influential individuals in the functional organization.

These criteria are important for the leader because this individual will most likely be responsible for politicking to get the best people on, or available as resources to, the team.

Not Minimizing Human Foibles

	Preimplementation	During Implementation
Troubleshooting		
Preventative Action	✓	

Self-Assessment Questions

1. Are assessment processes in place to profile employee behavior styles?
2. Are specialists available who can help employees adapt to new initiatives?
3. Is there a proven, organizational message that says, "It's okay to be human"?
4. Does the organization behave in ways that demonstrate to employees that they are extremely valuable resources?
5. Are human factors weighed equally with process issues in the design and implementation of initiatives?

If You Answered No, Beware! People will get hung up on the novelty of the initiative and not perform to their full potential.

WHAT NEEDS TO BE DONE?

Successfully implementing an initiative requires that the human asset be maximized. The organization must have a clear picture of its employee base—strengths and weaknesses—as weighed against the needs of the initiative. This assessment profiles employees as people with individual talents and frailties. Some of the elements that need to be considered include:

- Interpersonal styles.
- Personal values and beliefs.
- Expected, past group synergy.
- Influence of diversity issues on the workforce.
- Job satisfaction and career growth issues.
- Prevalent fears.

These factors need to be candidly assessed at the individual contributor, team, and organizational levels to determine their influence, positive and negative, on the initiative. They must be considered during:

- The design phase. Who will be involved in this phase? What human assets do they bring to the table in relationship to what is needed? Are there human capital issues that the design team needs to address during the design/pre-implementation phase? (See other Human Factor Barriers for more detail about specific issues.)
- The implementation phase. How do we accommodate human behavior in the organization at large? What kinds of training and other support will be needed to bring forth the best from all initiative participants?
- The maintenance phase. What needs to be done during this phase to ensure that the human asset continues to add value? Has enough attention been given to this phase?

Strategies should be developed to deal with each human element that might enhance or inhibit the success of initiative implementation.

WHY? WHAT ARE THE BENEFITS?

People are the engine of any initiative, and their "humanness" will influence how they react to the initiative. To plan for implementation without factoring this into the equation diminishes the probability of success.

In general, people are not trained in this aspect of initiative implementation, so it tends to be ignored. Designers are often more comfortable looking at the process issues and analytic information associated with the initiative and ignore the subtle, subjective, human relations issues that can influence implementation. There are few reliable approaches for evaluating humanness and mapping the present workforce. *Softer* issues, such as styles and diversity, lack objective guides. This makes it difficult for designers who are not trained in organizational behavior to second-guess what factors might impact the endeavor.

HOW? A RECIPE FOR ACTION

Categories of potential human impact (positive and negative) on the initiative must be identified. An assessment of all involved employees should be completed, and interventions planned to deal with the human influences. An example of how an initiative design team might approach the human element is shown in Table 1.

WHO? IN WHAT MANNER?

The design team must factor the human element into all initiative phases—design, implementation, and maintenance. Unless the team possesses the requisite skill to do this, an organizational behavior specialist and/or career counselor should be included as part of the team or called upon in a consulting/advisory role to assist the team.

TABLE 1

Addressing the Human Element

Human Element	Specific Variables	Assessment Approaches
Behavioral styles	• Approaches for dealing with the world at large. • Communication styles. • Comportment.	• Use of validated instruments to identify styles (may be self-reported and/or observer based).
Personal values and beliefs	• Personal norms. • Value systems.	• Use of attitude surveys. • Valuing exercises and instruments.
Group dynamics/ synergy	• Conflict management styles. • Decision-making styles. • Approach-avoidance behaviors. • Relationships—adult/adult, victim/persecutor/rescuer. • Preferred roles.	• Use of validated instruments to identify styles. • Interactive exercises and simulations to study behaviors within workshop settings (basis for behavior change).
Diversity	• Embracing differences. • Accommodating differences. • Recognition of specific differences present in the environment.	• Sensitivity and awareness training. • Diversity training. • Awareness instruments.
Job satisfaction and career growth	• Preferred work environments. • Willingness to take on new/extra/different assignments. • Ownership of career.	• Use of validated instruments to assess satisfaction and career interests. • Reliance on career counselors.
Fears	• Lack of risk taking. • Unwillingness to accept change. • Playing the "mind tapes"—need to be loved, need to be right, etc.	• Focused workshops to identify fears and plan actions to address them.

Relationship of Staff Competency to Initiative Success

	Preimplementation	During Implementation
Troubleshooting		
Preventative Action	✓	

Self-Assessment Questions

1. Do you regularly assess staff competencies?
2. Are you clear on the qualifications (technical and interpersonal) needed in those who will support future initiatives?
3. Has your organization aligned the competencies of its workforce to initiative needs? (What has been done in the past and how effective has it been?)
4. Does the organization have a clear methodology to identify required skills and a plan to maintain skill set currency?

If You Answered No, Beware! Enlisting the wrong people results in a poorly implemented initiative and an extremely frustrated workforce.

WHAT NEEDS TO BE DONE?

An improvement initiative is not a panacea for flaws in an organization. The success of any initiative is directly tied to the quality of performance of those involved in the endeavor. Too often organizations forget that they must look at the initiative's foundation. They must assess the availability of talent so that initiative requirements are aligned with the existing human resources.

Before considering an initiative, sponsors need to assess the skills and capabilities of those who will be involved. They should ask the question, "Do we have the appropriate people based on the requirements of the improvement tool we are considering?" The answer should assess both sides of the employee coin:

- *What is the quality of the management team?* Do they currently have the skills required to effectively manage in the new environment? Can they learn the new behaviors in a timely fashion? Are they willing to behave in different ways? (See Barrier 29: Lack of Competent, Assertive Management.)

For example, many organizations are implementing high-performance teams as a productivity tool. The requirements for managing in such an environment are quite different from those found in the traditional, hierarchical organization. Success is tied to the ability of those managing the new environment to operate in the flatter organization. Relying upon managers who cannot make the shift results in initiative failure.

- *What is the technical competency of the staff?* Has the organization made sure that the staff has current skills? Do they have the capacity to learn the new skills? There is a difference between a staff that has not been introduced to a new tool or technology and one that is incapable of migrating because technical requirements have changed drastically. Retooling the staff is not always feasible.

For example, an organization has a staff of general clerks and accountants who are proficient at expense allocations. It has been decided to introduce an improvement initiative. The tool relies upon sophisticated modeling techniques to forecast its expenses, with a focus on future implications. A staff with high school-level accounting/bookkeeping skills was able to handle the former requirements. However, the retraining needed to reach the skill level required after the redesign created a gap that could not be easily closed regardless of staff motivation.

The organization needs to include an assessment of job skills and staff competency as part of the initial analysis and evaluation of managerial tools. If a tool requires talent that is not available, the organization must make a decision:

- Do we retool our current staff?
- Do we start a new organization and phase out the old?

Selecting another tool that is better aligned with the talent available is not always possible. There is a constant need to update skills to meet changing business environment.

WHY? WHAT ARE THE BENEFITS?

Implementing managerial tools can require a quantum change in employee skill sets. Organizations need to jettison past methods and address marginal skills, either through retraining or restaffing. Finding people who believe in or are willing to function under the new initiative demands can be difficult.

This difficulty is highlighted by "greenfield" projects in which new organizations are started as a way to apply new managerial tools. There are documented cases in which thousands of people are interviewed to find the best few hundred to staff high-performance, team-based manufacturing plants. These numbers reflect how difficult it can be to find people who can properly apply the new tool.

The success of initiatives introduced in this way supports the importance of finding the right people; however, most organizations implement an initiative on top of current staff, which creates potential barriers to success before implementation is even attempted. At the crux of the problem of not using the right talent is the fact that most organizations don't address issues of:

- Counseling people on the new skill sets and identifying deficits.
- Publicly admitting that there is a lack of required talent within the community.

- Dealing with managers who are unable to downsize their workforce or cultivate the talent needed.

Many organizations ignore the gaps and shift people rather than retrain or replace them. The initiative is compromised if employee skill base is diluted. If it fails, the initiative will be blamed, the people issue will not be raised, and future initiatives will fall into the same trap.

HOW? A RECIPE FOR ACTION

The question needs to be asked, "Do we have the appropriate people for this initiative?" Initiative sponsors, with human resources assistance, need to identify the competencies and performance expectations required by the new tool. The team can benchmark best practices in other organizations and rely upon experts—in-house and external—to build the competency list. The chart in Table 1 provides a map for the macro assessment.

The matrix should be included as part of the design process. It can be a macro instrument early in the process; but as planning becomes more tactical, it should be refined to reassess specific competencies associated with newly formed positions.

In organizations that are unable to use a "greenfield" approach, the next step would be to look at current staff and determine matches and gaps in skill sets. Evaluate these gaps—can they be closed in a reasonable manner (in terms of time, cost, and resources)? Detailed training plans need to be developed, executed, and updated during the initiative's lifecycle.

TABLE 1

Competency Assessment Matrix

Competency	Assessment of Current Skills by Job Function	Responsibilities by Job Function with Clearly Defined New Performance Expectations	Degree of Severity of the Gaps	Degree of Control— Can You Do Something to Minimize the Gap?

A NOTE OF CAUTION: A danger exists that an apparent match at the macro level will prove to be a large or even insurmountable gap as the skills assessment becomes more detailed. What seemed logical in the beginning of the implementation process may not be feasible at the tactical level when competencies and people are paired.

WHO? IN WHAT MANNER?

The sponsoring team, with the help of the organization's change or training experts, must decide how to pursue the initiative with the current staff. This group will need to gather information about competencies. They will rely upon managers, individual contributors, and human resources to learn about current skill levels. Experts in the initiative will provide information about future competencies.

If there is the potential for personnel changes, it is important that human resources be involved throughout the process. If the organization is favoring retraining, it is important that the training staff be included in the assessment, design, and implementation phases.

Not Embracing Middle Management

	Preimplementation	During Implementation
Troubleshooting		
Preventative Action		✓

Self-Assessment Questions

1. Have past initiatives taken advantage of the expertise that can be provided by the middle-management team?
2. Is there a clear role for middle managers during initiative implementation?
3. Does the organization reinforce middle management's contribution to the endeavor?

If You Answered No, Beware! A corporate resource is lost and a potential pool of dissenters is created.

WHAT NEEDS TO BE DONE?

Every organization has a talent pool in its middle managers. It is the responsibility of initiative designers to carefully assess this potential leadership pool. How can the talents be applied to the envisioned environment? Can these managers fit the profile of the *new* leaders? The designers must be willing to quickly take advantage of the skills of middle managers by positioning them to participate in the leadership and management roles required in the new environment.

The danger is that, as the organization undergoes change, the middle manager can be considered a "dinosaur" and/or be ignored. The stereotype of the group is that it traditionally is opposed to change. In part this has been caused by:

- The fact that they rarely have been included in the process even though the change has had a direct impact on them.
- Their fear of being discharged because their roles cease to exist.

A solution is to embrace the group and make them an integral part of the transformation. Middle management can bring skills and business perspectives that add value to the endeavor.

The designers need to strategically position these people so that they are included in the process. Some roles that progressive organizations have identified for this group to fill include:

- Positioning them as advocates, experts, staff to draw upon their technical skills.
- Using them as coaches, mentors, and teachers (especially those who have new ideas) and drawing upon their managerial skills.
- Developing them into spokespersons and facilitators for the new initiative.

A NOTE OF CAUTION: Other, more traditional options for dealing with middle managers include:

- Re-incorporating them into work units as individual contributors.
- Moving them from managing people to managing projects.
- Terminating them.

These options are less desirable because the middle manager may be resistant to such roles and become an obstacle to implementation.

The role revision of middle management is difficult. The senior sponsors need to accurately assess these individuals and redefine their roles. The new roles need to be marketed so that everyone in the organization sees the value these individuals bring to the endeavor.

> **A NOTE OF CAUTION**: The organization at large may have difficulty relating to these people in new ways. Designers may define new roles for the middle manager, but the individuals dealing with the group don't acknowledge or respond to these new assignments. This exacerbates any wariness that formerly existed between line manager and subordinate.

WHY? WHAT ARE THE BENEFITS?

Many improvement initiatives are perceived as "employee participation" activities. This perception limits management involvement and ignores the role of middle managers. The omission of this group from any endeavor creates the potential for confrontation and dissension. A reason for their omission has historically been a lack of clarity about their role, a shift in job priorities, and a lack of training needed to develop the skills for the new environment. If inappropriately dealt with, middle managers are in a position to establish a tone in the organization that is contrary to the initiative's goals. When they are allowed to jeopardize the effort, people question the sincerity of those driving the initiative.

Part of the initiative design process must identify how middle managers can continue to be value-added contributors. Failure to view these individuals as valuable resources causes them to feel insecure. When these managers are unable to do well, they become frustrated and negatively affect the organization's productivity. By placing middle managers in new, progressive roles, the organization will utilize their talent in a positive manner. The shift of behavior that this pool demonstrates can drive the change.

HOW? A RECIPE FOR ACTION

Repositioning middle managers to maximize their contribution to the organization requires:

- Accurate assessment of their strengths and weaknesses. The purpose is to determine where to position them to take advantage of their talents.
- Review of the new organization with a focus on skill gaps. Seek areas where talent is lacking, where steps in the process remain undone and unassigned.
- "What-if" thinking about things that might be possible if people were available or recruited to do the work.
- Adequate training.
- Reinforcement of new behaviors to encourage mastery.

Senior managers, operationally responsible for the initiative, must champion what the middle manager can bring to bear on the endeavor. Changing leadership roles can be one of the hardest action items associated with any initiative. To be effective, senior managers must be prepared to make some hard assignment decisions (because egos can get involved) and willing to take forceful action to get middle managers who can perform effectively in the new roles. The considerations that gain alignment are outlined by the columns in the grid shown in Table 1.

TABLE 1

Aligning Middle-Management Talent with Organizational Needs

Skill/ Competency That Is Needed in the New Organization	Middle Managers Who Possess the Skill or Competency—Ranked by Degree of Mastery			Actions Specific Middle Managers Must Demonstrate to Show That Skill Is Present/Has Been Attained		Behaviors in Middle Management That Hinder Performance in the New Environment	
	High	Medium	Low	Action	Person	Behavior	Person(s)

The information captured by the grid assesses current middle managers and provides a development tool that senior managers can use to coach these individuals. Once the assessment has been completed, senior managers need to hold discussions with middle managers to help them finalize and gain ownership of their "new" role. Operational efficiency will require that the model for assessing and assigning be applicable to other targeted employee groups.

WHO? IN WHAT MANNER?

Taking action regarding the re-appointment of middle managers is the responsibility of the senior manager. Required competencies for new positions can be identified by the initiative's design team, generally with the assistance of the middle managers themselves. Experts who understand the initiative's requirements and are skilled in developing competency/skill maps may be called upon as resources. Once the new criteria for middle managers have been established, it becomes the responsibility of the controlling management body to make decisions regarding the role of each individual middle manager within the new environment.

Not Fostering Creative, Visionary Thinking

	Preimplementation	During Implementation
Troubleshooting		
Preventative Action	✓	

Self-Assessment Questions

1. Is creativity encouraged in your organization?
2. Can you name/describe the last truly creative, broad-based idea that was implemented within the organization?
3. Are creative thinkers acclaimed throughout your organization? Are their contributions acknowledged/prized?
4. Are people positioned within the organization to ensure that creative ideas are evaluated carefully and not discounted because they are different?

If You Answered No, Beware! Futuristic thinking needed to make the organization competitive in a rapidly changing world doesn't surface.

WHAT NEEDS TO BE DONE?

Organizations that are going to successfully implement initiatives must embrace creative thinking and innovation. This type of thinking represents a part of the mix (analytical, cheerleading, administrative, and creative) needed to make any initiative work. Points at which creativity is necessary include:

- Pre-initiative—this is the thinking that allows someone to envision the future and how the proposed initiative will make a difference to business performance.
- Planning phase—this is the thinking that allows people to break out of the mold to see different ways to operate more effectively and to incorporate the initiative into daily business operations.
- Post-implementation—this is the thinking that sustains momentum and fosters continuous improvement of the initiative. It positions the organization to "ride the waves" (that is, to maximize the crest of the initiative and know when to integrate with future initiatives).

Initiative sponsors need to recognize the importance of creative thinking. Employees who exhibit it need to be acknowledged and embraced by the initiative core team and senior management. It is critical that they not be squeezed back into the box. These individuals need to be visible so that the organization at large recognizes that creativity is acceptable—even required—thinking.

WHY? WHAT ARE THE BENEFITS?

The "creative thinking" asset is fairly limited in most traditional organizations. (Start-up, young, product-development organizations tend to encourage this type of thinker and they tend to rely more on these patterns.) Organizations that don't capitalize on creativity don't get the greatest return on the investment of resources into initiatives. Those thoroughly enmeshed in the old thinking have difficulty seeing the potential applicability of new initiatives. The more "mature" the organization gets, the more difficult it is for change to occur and for new initiatives to be successfully implemented.

Organizations need to identify and encourage mavericks who "look for new opportunities" so that the firm doesn't expend energy getting very good at things that no longer add sufficient value. The organization also needs to capitalize on the visionary thinker—the person who is able to look at the situation and see a higher level of innovation and potential. This ensures that the organization remains on the cutting edge and sets the pace within its industry.

A NOTE OF CAUTION: To be most effective the truly visionary thinker needs to be paired with a more innovative person who is better able to operationalize ideas.

HOW? A RECIPE FOR ACTION

Initiative success often depends upon the talents of creative individuals being fully realized. It is the senior manager's responsibility to pave the way for these individuals so that their contributions can be realized. To do so they must:

- *Nurture them*—that is, find ways to encourage their creative thinking.
- *Recognize their contributions* so that they are willing to present new ideas.

A NOTE OF CAUTION: Restricting individuals' thinking will force them underground to implement their ideas covertly or drive them to other organizations that are more supportive.

- *Take the risk to support them.* The organization must visibly support creative thinkers by implementing their recommendations and/or providing company resources to develop their ideas. (Corporate reality is that not every idea will be serviceable; however, a certain percentage of ideas must be implemented to ensure that innovation continues.)
- *Expand.* Use structured approaches, to stimulate creative thinking. An example is Dr. Edward de Bono's Six Hat Thinking method, which encourages individuals to assume different mindsets, or "hats," when dealing with a challenge. By reviewing a situation from different perspectives alternative solutions can emerge. Such tools can make

everyone more creative, or at least lead them to appreciate such skills in others.

Taking these steps will establish the organization as a safe environment for creative thinking. Everyone should be encouraged to develop/appreciate this trait.

WHO? IN WHAT MANNER?

The senior manager in the business unit is responsible for providing support for creative ventures. Creative thinkers need ongoing reinforcement that acknowledges their contribution. Who the supporters are will depend upon the type of thinking, the scope of thinking, and the hierarchical position of the individual.

Managers need to be trained on structured approaches to creative thinking. They need to designate specific time for employees to creatively resolve work issues and further develop their creativity skills.

Not Confronting the Resistance to the Initiative

	Preimplementation	During Implementation
Troubleshooting	✓	
Preventative Action		

Self-Assessment Questions

1. Does your organization have a strategy to confront resistance to the initiative?
2. Have you analyzed the reasons for resistance?
3. In the past have you pinpointed overt and/or covert sources of resistance to endeavors?

If You Answered No, Beware! Left unchallenged, those who resist encourage others to do the same.

WHAT NEEDS TO BE DONE?

In most cases when an initiative meets resistance, something is wrong with the process and it needs to be addressed. Statistics suggest that 85% of all problems are indeed problems with the initiative itself. In the other 15%, the problem lies with employees (issues of defiance or saturation) and needs to be dealt with as a performance management issue.

Whenever an initiative is introduced, there will be employees who will resist it. The challenge is for the company to recognize, assess and respond quickly and effectively to such obstructions. Resistance does not reveal what is faulty, but it does signal that something is not working. A thorough review is required. When obstacles emerge, the initiative leaders must listen and examine the concerns.

Not all resentment will be obvious. It is essential for the organization to identify the warning signs that indicate employees' lack of receptivity to or capacity to deal with the new effort. Some signs are listed in Table 1.

WHY? WHAT ARE THE BENEFITS?

Employees tend to focus on how the initiative will affect them personally. If they feel negative about the endeavor and these feelings are kept covert, the organization will have difficulty getting them to buy in. Employees will expend infinite amounts of energy replaying their concerns and fears. This reduces organizational performance.

TABLE 1

Signs of Nonreceptivity to the Initiative

- Discussions in informal gathering spots.
- Increased absenteeism.
- Elevated number of work injuries.
- Heightened amount of canceled appointments.
- Inability to schedule meetings.
- Minimized participation in meetings.
- General inertia and inappropriate interpersonal reactions.

Positively managing resistance assists the company in institutionalizing the initiative. If not managed, the resistance becomes etched—taken for granted—and becomes accepted behavior in the organization. Once resistance is ingrained, skepticism spreads and damages the attainment of initiative goals.

HOW? A RECIPE FOR ACTION

During the implementation phase, the project team will need to measure employee attitudes. This review should be done informally and with different levels and functional groups. It signals to the workforce that the organization is sensitive to their feelings.

The company should not criticize concerned individuals who raise issues—this will discount the input and limit future participation. The company should address the problem by seeking opinions and using gathered information to improve the process.

Once the reasons for the resistance have been carefully described, the project team should use problem-solving techniques to identify root causes and develop solutions to address the resistance and elevate comfort levels. Table 2 presents solutions to some typical concerns.

The sponsoring team needs to constantly remind people of the benefits of the endeavor and establish vehicles for employees to air issues and obstacles.

It is equally imperative to get employees to partake in the effort—acceptance frequently comes through doing. The earlier the workforce can provide input to the implementation process, the more likely employees will understand its direction and be willing to accept it.

WHO? IN WHAT MANNER?

The implementation team is positioned to identify resistance to the initiative in its early stages. Team members need a set of skills that will allow them to note resistance and confront it. Specific expectations for the team include:

- They will learn how individual managers intend to implement the effort and how specific groups are expected to

TABLE 2

Possible Solutions to Resistance

Possible Concerns	Solutions
Initiative implementation is too fast	▪ Change timetable so that it is at a pace the company can accept. ▪ Bring in temps to augment staff during the transition process. ▪ Provide training on time management.
Scope of initiative is too broad; too much changing at one time	▪ Reduce scope of initiative, or focus on one critical success factor or one business unit at a time. ▪ Help individuals with goal and priority setting processes.
Initiative is very different from existing fundamental principles and practices	▪ Identify those aspects of the existing principles that are similar to the endeavor and use the similarities to link the two approaches.
See the effort as a "loss" of existing behaviors and methodologies	▪ Hold a service where the "loss" can be enshrined. ▪ Provide training on dealing with the change and loss cycles.
Initiative's philosophy appears to be inappropriate for a specific business or work unit	▪ Use WIIFM's to communicate the effort from unit's point of view so that they see value (see Barrier 19: Not Understanding That Everyone Wants to Know: What's in it For Me?).
Employees' tolerance level for change is ignored	▪ Focus on change process at human level. Provide stress management training. ▪ Develop managers' sensitivity to employees' capacity for change.
Employees do not understand the expectations of the endeavor	▪ Illustrate the initiative three distinct ways. ▪ Use analogies, situations, stories, and demonstrations to increase understanding.

respond. They can gather this information by listening, observation, and questioning managers and employees.

▪ They are forthright and gain the esteem and assistance of workgroups. These individuals will facilitate conversations between different people with various perspectives.

- They possess the observation skills to note subtle exchanges of information and beliefs as employees discuss and respond to the change.
- They demonstrate analytical and problem-solving skills to determine the action that will need to be taken. They also need these skills to conclude if a specific process step should be delayed and/or modified because the workgroup is not ready for the transformation.
- They are familiar with collaborative change management techniques.

READING 35–1

A nonprofit firm found that the best way to deal with resisters was to include them in the design team for all proposed initiatives. The individuals had the opportunity to voice their concerns and ensure that they were addressed. Involvement resulted in buy-in—these individuals frequently became the greatest proponents of the proposed change.

No Time for the Initiative

	Preimplementation	During Implementation
Troubleshooting		✓
Preventative Action		

Self-Assessment Questions

1. Do employees understand and own the initiative process?
2. Is hands-on experience used early in the initiative implementation?
3. Is the organization improving the workforce's ability to learn and apply knowledge?

If You Answered No, Beware! The initiative, being ignored, becomes a effort "on paper" only.

WHAT NEEDS TO BE DONE?

The volume of work being produced by business units is steadily increasing in an atmosphere of doing more—and doing it better, faster, and cheaper. Overburdened employees feel increased pressure when a new endeavor is introduced. When they are not involved in an initiative's design, it is harder for them to understand how it can be of benefit. Without hands-on experience, the workforce fears the initiative. As a result, it is easier for them to focus on the "real" work they have to get done immediately; they ignore the initiative and hope it will go away.

Sponsors need to create a sense of ownership for the initiative. The process of institutionalizing the initiative must be established and understood by both the implementors and the workforce at large. The process begins with awareness of the need to learn about the initiative, which is developed by sponsors. Initiatives should promote a system of learning that runs in tandem with and doesn't hinder the execution of daily operations. A first step is to make it safe for employees to confess their lack of knowledge about the initiative and its requirements for new skills. Initiatives generally require employees to exert effort beyond that required to meet their daily work quotas. They must see the initiative as a positive learning experience which furthers their ability to solve daily operational problems and makes them more efficient and marketable. This linkage accelerates the transfer of knowledge and the application of initiative principles. It minimizes the view that the initiative takes extra time, which in turn causes employees to avoid involvement.

WHY? WHAT ARE THE BENEFITS?

Employees are quick to view an initiative as additional responsibility. They are troubled by the unknown. Some typical fears they experience:

- How much new knowledge is needed?
- Will I be capable of learning it?
- Will I have the time to learn it?

- What will be the reprimand for errors?
- What will be the repercussions of ignoring the initiative?

Workgroup acceptance of the initiative is shaped over time. Without true understanding and ownership of the endeavor, there is minimal commitment and effort. Failure of initiatives has been tied to a lack of information and knowledge about them. Learning must take place before people can own an initiative. Investments in learning can mold the way employees think about the endeavor and their work: "Will the initiative help me do a better job, or is it just one more thing that gets in the way of my doing what they pay me to do?"

Most people learn from experience, and when workers become involved with the initiative they gain understanding. Using the work unit as a learning laboratory leads to greater practical application of the initiative. This approach combines employee experience with a set of pragmatic tools. Employees are more accepting because the initiative engages their existing talents and adds new job skills and knowledge.

HOW? A RECIPE FOR ACTION

Educate the workforce about how the initiative works as an entire system. Provide hands-on experience that allows employees to understand the initiative in a nonthreatening way.

- One approach is to create role plays, work simulations, or demonstrations to illustrate the principles of the initiative and get employees to experience aspects of the initiative in a non-work setting. Practical applications in a safe environment create enthusiasm and involvement.
- Another method is to apply the concepts directly within the work setting. Identify the systematically relevant errors that recur daily. Apply the initiative's concept to map out the true problem and alternative solutions. This enhances understanding and ownership of the endeavor.

WHO? IN WHAT MANNER?

Everyone in the organization needs to participate in the learning process. Involved parties and their roles are as follows:

- Managers and sponsors need to understand the importance of, allocate resources for, and promote ongoing learning. They should look for operational opportunities that create learning situations.
- Employees need to see the organization from a broader perspective—from the managers', customers', initiative sponsors', and implementors' viewpoints. They also need to be open to and accept criticism about the business and ways to improve it.

READING 36–1

A medical services organization underwent a total redesign effort. Once people were positioned in their new jobs, an undercurrent of dissatisfaction arose around the conflict between trying to do work in the new way and still meet production quotas. Senior management continually reinforced the importance of adopting new techniques through the hiring of temps to allow for cross-training and classroom time, reinforcing actions that supported the new model, and stepping in to help meet quotas.

Avoiding Performance Management Issues

	Preimplementation	During Implementation
Troubleshooting		✓
Preventative Action		

Self-Assessment Questions

1. Are there written performance goals associated with each position?
2. Would you characterize your organization as one that holds members accountable for their performance?
3. Only those who perform at acceptable performance standard levels are allowed to remain in the organization?

If You Answered No, Beware! The poor performers bring down productivity and dampen the enthusiasm of the entire group.

WHAT NEEDS TO BE DONE?

Performance management refers to the actions taken by managers and team members to ensure that each person performs to further organizational and team productivity and relationships. Initiatives frequently require new sets of behaviors and/or skills. Unless performance expectations are established and those in charge manage according to those expectations, the initiative will not succeed. Preceding the implementation process, a set of performance standards needs to be made public. Each employee must agree to them and understand that inappropriate behavior will be addressed and managed.

WHY? WHAT ARE THE BENEFITS?

Everyone involved needs to recognize the importance of performing (technically and interpersonally) in a way that supports the goals of the initiative. If management is not willing to define performance goals or deal with "hard" management issues, initiatives may be instituted in hopes that the inadequate performers will choose to leave. This is an inappropriate expectation for an initiative.

Employees are not easily fooled and they are aware of performance management problems within an organization. They lose respect for the initiative and its implementors when the endeavor is a disguise for dealing with core performance problems that no one wants to address. Being clear about what is expected and managing performance to that level enhances productivity and morale. Individuals like to know their boundaries and that everyone will be held accountable for the same standard. In such an environment, people are motivated, perform well and have a higher degree of respect for managers and peers.

HOW? A RECIPE FOR ACTION

Begin by determining what performance expectations will be required as a result of the initiative. It is the responsibility of the design team to present concrete role and responsibility descriptions for jobs in the new organization. Some ways to assemble this information include:

- Detail each job. Develop a job description, thinking in terms of what you might need for internal job posting, for outside recruiting, or for a presentation to management to justify a new or upgraded position.
- Develop lists or tables of the necessary skills (a model for such a table is shown in Table 1). Categorize by type of skills (i.e., technical job skills, interpersonal skills, leadership/management skills), then develop a detailed description listing the specific activities, accountabilities, and outcomes of the job tasks by function and job title.

Explore the availability and validity of commercially developed packages that focus on the skills and competencies required of employees in your industry or function. When available they can simplify and speed up the process of skill identification and assessment. Check into the opportunity to customize the packages. Do their input options (paper and pencil, on-line) match your organizational needs? You might consider benchmarking other organizations that have lists of skills required for environments such as the one you are designing. This can jump-start your process or act as a reality check for material that you have developed.

A NOTE OF CAUTION: You may find resistance to information sharing. Some organizations on the leading edge of job redesign consider the information a competitive advantage.

TABLE 1

Skill and Performance Expectations for New Jobs

Job—Generic Definition	Associated Skills by Category			New Performance Expectations	
	Technical	Interpersonal	Leadership/ Managerial	Function and Job Title	Description of Primary Activities, Accountabilities, and Outcomes

Once the skills requirements for the new environment have been established, individual performance expectations can be defined. Ways of gathering this information include:

- 360° input on expected performance—individual, manager, team mates, and customers all provide expectations for the position.
- Self-evaluation—provide check sheets of skills and have new incumbents share their perceptions of the requirements of the newly designed position, providing information about skills and expected performance levels.
- Manager evaluation—determine what management expects in the way of performance.

WHO? IN WHAT MANNER?

Meeting performance expectations is the responsibility of the manager. The initiative design team and human resource personnel should work together to identify expected and/or required skills and behaviors. Including a cross-section of employees in the skill description development process improves satisfaction with performance expectations, encourages increased adherence to those expectations, and results in less resistance to corrective action when expectations are not met.

READING 37–1

A real estate developer needed to maintain market share. The organization formed a task force and, with the help of a consultant, reassessed job requirements for all positions. Each employee met with the owner to identify skill gaps. Performance contracts were written to identify specific skill development needs, to determine how the skills were to be developed, and by when.

ORGANIZATIONAL ISSUES

Providing the Foundation and Framework for the Initiative

	Preimplementation	During Implementation
Troubleshooting	40. Informal organizational structures are sabotaging the effort. 41. Unofficial norms and procedures impact the success of the initiative. 47. Not recognizing customer needs.	42. Not considering the coordination costs. 43. Not making use of hard data. 46. Ineffective evaluation methods. 48. Ineffectual performance appraisals. 49. Lack of appropriate training methodologies. 50. Allowing inefficient meetings.
Preventative Action	38. Inappropriate reliance on the model. 39. Lack of understanding of formal organizational systems.	44. Compensation and rewards are not aligned with the initiative. 45. Lack of recognition for small achievements.

The organization can be viewed as a whole; it can also be viewed as the systems and structures that comprise the whole. If these parts are not interconnected, the company has difficulty achieving its goals. Organizational design and hierarchy provides a framework for integrating the various systems and structures. How well the design functions depends on its appropriateness to the targeted goals and the response of the workforce to the design. Within the architecture are formal, informal, official, and unofficial systems and structures that affect employee behavior.

When leveraging an initiative, it is important for leaders to understand and recognize how these interdependent connections can affect the endeavor. Initiative leaders improve their chances of success if they align the endeavor to new or existing systems and structures. They need to gain insight into the official and unofficial operating processes, norms, and procedures and the reactions of different audiences to the design. If responses are positive, employees will be more willing to embrace the initiative.

One clear reason why initiatives fail is that there are competing forces within the organization. A complex and unstable design increases the difficulty of coordinating the endeavor. If the existing norms, systems, structures, and procedures conflict with the direction of the initiative, integration cannot be obtained. Insuring that the architecture is sound and properly aligned will increase the probability of initiative success.

Inappropriate Reliance on the Model

	Preimplementation	During Implementation
Troubleshooting		
Preventative Action	✓	

Self-Assessment Questions

1. Have you determined if the model is appropriate for the organization?
2. Will people in the organization react positively to the initiative model?
3. Are designers willing to customize the model to meet the specific needs of the organization?
4. Do people treat the model as a framework rather than as gospel?

If You Answered No, Beware! The model may become the end rather than the means.

WHAT NEEDS TO BE DONE?

The purpose of undertaking an initiative is to improve the organization's performance. It is not to ensure "perfect" implementation of a managerial tool. The designers must provide a sense of balance to prevent situations where the initiative's framework is over- or underemphasized. The goal is to keep the model from being counterproductive by becoming more important than the work being supported.

Choosing an initiative model necessitates rigor being applied. The initiative methodology provides a framework so that the endeavor can succeed as envisioned. The model should strengthen the capabilities of the organization. It should provide the workforce with a map of how to achieve the company's goals. The implementation team is responsible for providing information about how the model works. Before doing this, the team needs to validate their interpretation of the methodology so they are not recommending incorrect concepts or procedures.

It is important that the organization choose the correct managerial tool, tailor it to meet its needs, and define how the intervention will operate. Companies can begin their research by asking:

- Are we doing it exactly as other organizations have?
- Do we need to tweak it to make it work?

The management team is responsible for setting realistic boundaries for applying the initiative model. Beginning the process with a very clear picture of expectations for the new environment—in terms of behavior, output, and organization—is critical to effective implementation. Within established boundaries and scope, work units have the flexibility to either apply or not apply elements based on their knowledge of the workplace, the competitive environment, customers' unmet needs, and the work being done.

WHY? WHAT ARE THE BENEFITS?

Initiatives are intentional, organized disruptions; therefore, they will encounter obstacles. The more appropriate the initiatives, the more dynamic it will make the organization.

Research shows that too many initiatives have been poorly applied. They have been used for narrow purposes, or their capabilities were not aligned to the organization's needs and goals. Without diagnosing both the elements of the model and the root causes of organizational obstacles to be overcome, implementation will be less than optimum.

HOW? A RECIPE FOR ACTION

Initiative designers need to spend time studying potential initiative models. They need to benchmark other organizations' approaches and decide how they will incorporate them. This evaluation identifies the key components of the model and assesses the suitability of the model to the organization. A charting approach can identify the fitness of a model and its potential impact on the organization. The chart shown in Table 1 helps to organize and interpret the parameters of a model and provides information on how it might be implemented.

Assessing the answers to the questions in Table 1 will reveal the appropriateness of a model being considered for implementation. This comparative approach will develop a clear picture of the match between the initiative being evaluated and the assessors' environment. The responses provide information that the implementation team will need to reference when designing the initiative. The chart challenges the team to think through the organization's reason for selecting the model and to consider the changes—subtle and obvious—that will be needed in the organization to make the initiative work.

WHO? IN WHAT MANNER?

The senior managers need to make sure that they are clear about: the model, the organization's constraints around the model, the impact of changes to the model on implementation, and strategic direction of the organization. Who is involved in the process of gaining this information will be dependent upon the organization's knowledge, sophistication and existing structure.

TABLE 1

Evaluation of Model Parameters

Parameters	Answers—What Does It Look Like, and How Will It Fit?	
	Generic—Drawn From Our Research and Comparisons	Our Organization—Based on Our Culture and Norms
1. Model—a brief description.		
2. What is the reason for the initiative?		
3. How have other organizations used this model?		
4. Will the model help us reach our organizational goals?		
5. Will the initiative cause a standstill or paradigm shift?		
6. What amount/scale of change will the initiative cause?		
7. What strategy will be used to heighten the model's effectiveness?		
8. What planning is needed to make the model work within the organization?		
9. Are there any aspects of the model we particularly like? Do not like? Why?		
10. How long has it typically taken to fully implement this model?		
11. Will this model enhance productivity here?		
12. Does the model match the business needs, people, and changing environment?		

Some senior managers conduct the research themselves, which increases the likelihood that they will embrace and promote the initiative. (See Barrier 25.)

Other senior managers may commission a team to conduct the research and make recommendations on how to apply the model appropriately. After the recommendations are presented, the senior managers need to probe and evaluate whether the model will meet the changing business conditions and the strategic direction of the organization.

If the key decision makers lack the knowledge to clarify the initiative's impact, they may need to seek outside support, which might come from initiative experts or from contacts in other companies that have adopted the initiative.

Lack of Understanding of Formal Organizational Systems

	Preimplementation	During Implementation
Troubleshooting		
Preventative Action	✓	

Self-Assessment Questions

1. Do initiative sponsors understand the formal organizational systems that are in place—what they are and how they operate?
2. Does the organization adequately control its formal systems?
3. Does the organization have a mechanism in place to address key concerns of employees about the current systems?
4. Have formal systems been revamped to promote the initiative?

If You Answered No, Beware! Not understanding and using formal systems severely limits the probability of the initiative being integrated into the organization.

WHAT NEEDS TO BE DONE?

The formal systems of any organization—policies, problem management, decision-making structures, compensation, rewards and recognition—need to be aligned with and support the goals of the organization's initiatives. Organizations must understand how their systems are integrated and look for links to the initiative. Before introducing an initiative, a company should evaluate its formal systems, knowing that there might be a need to transform or revise them.

A comprehensive review of formal systems must include employee perceptions about the current systems, not just those of managers and organizational development specialists. The company needs to observe and document current system functionality and assess its impact on organizational performance. It also needs to determine which systems, if any, conflict with the effort's goals and modify them so that they are aligned.

WHY? WHAT ARE THE BENEFITS?

Out of the need to compete, organizations sometimes attempt to implement initiatives without understanding the formal organization within which they will be integrated. Formal structures reflect what is important to the managers who create them and identify behaviors that are valued within the organization. The company must align the goals of the endeavor with those of formal systems. If there is disagreement, employees receive conflicting messages and respond by ignoring the directives of the initiative, becoming immobilized, or creating their own informal systems to deal with the ambiguity.

Formal systems are not optional; they must not be willfully overlooked or ignored during the execution of an initiative. Some companies treat the initiative as a separate entity and fail to tie it to the formal systems. These firms make no attempt to redesign their formal systems to support the initiative. When there is a lack of integration, the initiative becomes detached, fails to gain credibility, and tends to be implemented as a parallel structure. The discrepancies are viewed as conflicts between the two structures and thus nurture employee resistance to change.

HOW? A RECIPE FOR ACTION

To understand formal systems, companies need to analyze how they currently function. Before assessment, check to see that senior managers have:

- Clearly communicated the goals of the assessment, how it should be conducted, and who is on the team.
- Defined the desired results.
- Ensured that the team is sensitive to the potential impact on the workforce of changes to the formal systems.

The grid shown in Table 1 provides a map that the design team can use to assess the current systems. It has been completed with text that reflects the stages of adoption used by a company moving towards a team-based, empowered organization. Steps to follow are shown in Table 2.

WHO? IN WHAT MANNER?

The executive managers need to sanction the system evaluation process and establish a team of respected managers to assess the current organizational systems against the future state the initiative is driving toward.

Due to the tension that may arise in this assessment and recommendation process, comprehensive training on group dynamics and negotiating skills is strongly suggested. If the organization does not have a qualified individual on staff to conduct this training, an outside third party may be engaged.

TABLE 1

Formal Organizational Systems Evaluation

Formal Organization Systems	Development Stages			
	Wonder	Early Stages	Understanding	Clear Evidence
Problem management	Problems are handled as they occur; finger-pointing; no clear direction	Tracking system is established to record problems; long-term solutions are not identified	Communication is shared openly regarding problems and resolutions sought; creative thinking permitted	Problems are prevented before they occur; all work groups are open to suggestions from others for improvement; creative thinking inspired
Norms and procedures	Rigid rules	Some flexibility with rules	Greater autonomy with rules	Rules modified to meet customer needs
Compensation	Pay by seniority or cost of living; no incentives	Pay for individual skills; occasional workgroup incentives	Pay for individual skills; some workgroup incentives	Balance of pay for knowledge, results as accountabilities, and workgroup performance
Rewards and recognition	Inordinate reinforcement for management, none for workforce	Most privileges for management, some rewards for workforce	Shared recognition for both management and employees	Equality of recognition for entire population
Decision-making structures	Autocratic management; top-down directives; no patience for mistakes—management alone makes decisions	Less domineering management; lateral communication forming; some patience for mistakes—management requests input	Participatory management, two-way and lateral communication encouraged—employees become group with managers and make joint decisions	No communication barriers; shared authority to make decisions—decision-making authority rests with whoever needs it based on business issues

189

TABLE 2

Steps to Assess Current Formal Systems

1. Determine the present stage for each of the organization's formal systems (a sampling is provided in the grid).
2. Compare the criteria of where your system is today against where it should be.
3. Analyze the gaps and brainstorm potential changes in your current systems that could be employed to align each system with the initiative.
4. Examine the data and decide which system modifications will be easiest to implement with minimal negative effects. This usually leads to "quick wins," which encourage individuals to tackle more demanding system modifications.
5. Develop specific action plans to help you achieve your desired state.
6. Discuss plans with the workforce so they can begin to understand the need for change. Employees should be involved in the process so that they contribute and become accountable for the execution.
7. Recommend to senior managers that they align the endeavor and close gaps between present and desired formal systems. Senior management must be open to recommendations and ensure that timely action will occur after the presentation of the suggestions or empower the group to act on their behalf.

BARRIER

Informal Organizational Structures Are Sabotaging the Effort

	Preimplementation	During Implementation
Troubleshooting	✔	
Preventative Action		

Self-Assessment Questions

1. Are you aware of the crucial informal relationships that exist within the company?
2. Have you evaluated the informal structure to determine impacts on business performance?
3. Have the informal structures impeded past initiative implementation? If so, do you know how, why, and what to do about it?
4. Do you know what information the informal networks can provide about the adoption of initiative that the formal hierarchy cannot?

If You Answered No, Beware! The organization will have only limited ability to effectively intercede in these structures to refocus energy on the initiative.

WHAT NEEDS TO BE DONE?

Some organizations have difficulty admitting that informal networks have as much power as they do. Other organizations are uncomfortable tapping into these channels. However, charting the informal relationships highlights opportunities for enhancing support for the effort. It is important that initiative leaders, sponsors, champions, and implementation team members acknowledge and manage these relationships.

Organizations need to understand and accept the power of informal networks. They should define these networks and build on their collective potential. Sponsors can tap into these networks, creating new relationships and challenging the old. When sponsors identify the important individuals in the informal hierarchy, they can focus their energies on establishing bonds with these key people. They can market the initiative from the key individuals' perspective and thus effectively administer the endeavor as a collaborative process and integrate it in a unified manner.

WHY? WHAT ARE THE BENEFITS?

Every organization implementing an initiative is faced with the need to challenge opposing forces and build new perspectives. In many organizations conflicts flare because the informal structures are neglected. The power of these networks can demolish the chance for the initiative to be adopted. The attitudes of highly influential individuals within the informal hierarchy can impact the initiative—either intentionally, to discredit the new idea, or accidentally due to a lack of understanding about the initiative.

Initiative leaders need to accept that these relationships do exist. They need to understand that some employees, because of their informal roles, can have more effect on the buy-in of the initiative than do their managers. Furthermore, employees sometimes disregard instructions from those instituting the endeavor based on these informal allegiances. By harnessing the informal networks, initiative sponsors can influence perceptions of the organization and improve the initiative's probability of success.

HOW? A RECIPE FOR ACTION

The first step in identifying the informal hierarchy is to acknowledge that it exists. Then its structure needs to be documented. This allows initiative planners to understand and view its span of control. It is important to look beyond the surface contacts to get a true picture of the informal networks. This may necessitate investigation by observing relationships at informal gathering spots, exploring possible connections with trusted co-workers, and talking to people.

> A sociogram is a tool that is frequently used to map interpersonal relationships within an organization.

Begin the documentation by deciding who has the informal authority over each of the core business processes. Then determine who these key individuals interact with, frequently communicate with, and confide in. What are the power relationships? How do they influence jobs and employee behavior? Look at several levels, up, down, and across the organization.

> Create a chart reflecting these interrelationships. One technique is to give employees general parameters for describing their work relationships and have them illustrate the work unit or organization as they see it.

Next, review past change efforts, which are valuable sources of information regarding the informal channels. Select criteria for comparative analysis; for example:

- Determine who supported and who impeded the past endeavors—look for patterns.
- Examine hierarchical positions and relationships—review multiple levels and functions.
- Compare data from several charts—look for patterns.

This analysis helps to identify those who may have the strongest motivation to either endorse or challenge the new effort. Verify the data with additional observation and conversations.

Use the summarized information from the various methods to predict the typical reactions each informal network will have toward the current initiative. By understanding the endeavor from each network's perspective, initiative leaders can plan specific approaches to gain acceptance for the effort.

WHO? IN WHAT MANNER?

Three groups of people are concerned with information related to the informal organization:

- People who design the framework and collect the data. They need to be skilled in organizational behavior and data-collection techniques. If this is not possible, the organization needs to retain neutral, outside observers.
- Individuals throughout the organization who will be interviewed to provide the information about the actual informal networks. It is critical to involve enough people to guarantee an accurate picture.
- Implementation team members who have to use the data to accomplish the initiative's integration into the organization.

Unofficial Norms and Procedures Impact the Success of the Initiative

	Preimplementation	During Implementation
Troubleshooting	✓	
Preventative Action		

Self-Assessment Questions

1. Do you know what your unofficial norms are? Are they common to the entire organization?
2. Have you assessed how employee behaviors influence the informal procedures and norms?
3. Have you analyzed the influence of informal procedures and norms on the initiative?
4. Do you have a plan to balance informal procedures and norms with the organization's strategies?

If You Answered No, Beware! Lack of control of these variables inhibits rewriting the rules so the initiative can flourish.

WHAT NEEDS TO BE DONE?

Informal procedures and norms set operational boundaries and signal to employees the behaviors to be adopted. Employees are aware of which actions get rewarded, who gets reprimanded, how risk taking is viewed, and when favoritism is tolerated. They learn the "correct" procedures and norms by analyzing current practices.

Employees feel varying degrees of pressure from these procedures and norms. It is important to understand their influence on the various workgroups within the company. Observe and interview the workforce to gather this information, then apply it throughout the initiative's lifecycle to guide implementation decisions and to serve as a litmus test for the appropriateness of plans.

WHY? WHAT ARE THE BENEFITS?

Unofficial procedures and norms which go unnoticed in organizations can inhibit the execution of the initiative. This leads to confusion and mixed messages, encouraging a lack of responsiveness and commitment from the workforce.

For the endeavor to succeed, norms and procedures must complement the new principles and behaviors. Employees cannot be allowed to surreptitiously follow unofficial procedures. Assess the variables that either support or hinder the effort, then either incorporate or terminate specific norms and procedures accordingly. Changing the regulations lets employees know which new behaviors will be acceptable and reinforced.

HOW? A RECIPE FOR ACTION

To identify the procedures and norms:

- Brainstorm lists of unofficial norms and procedures that are currently in place.
- Have employees describe via role playing how things get done and how people behave.
- Conduct surveys or interviews to gather information about current practices.

Once the initial information is gathered, clarify and identify the immediate impact of each procedure and norm on specific workgroups, locations, and the company as a whole. Review the data against a preset list of initiative conditions/expectations and determine relationships of norms and procedures to organization, to initiative. Decide what, if anything, needs to change. Some questions to ask are shown in Table 1.

Once the questions have been answered, prioritize the information. Pay special attention to differences by workgroup and location.

- Test the validity of the data by conducting informal interviews with employees. A good place to hold these discussions is at the casual gathering places where employees assemble.
- Pinpoint ways to adjust the unofficial norms and procedures to reinforce the behavior the company is trying to instill. Each possible alternative should be analyzed to determine the impacts of the changes.
- Complete Table 2 to generate ideas for modifying the procedures.

> **Unofficial Norm:** Seek upward growth.
>
> **Initiative Need:** Lateral moves to gain broader operational knowledge.
>
> **Workforce Perception:** Employees perceive lateral moves as negative.
>
> **Modification:** Visibly reward individuals who take lateral moves.

TABLE 1

Variables to Assess Readiness for Change

1. What are the unofficial norms and procedures of each workgroup?
2. Are there any hidden agendas behind them? What are they?
3. How does employee behavior reflect these procedures? Note differences based on group and location.
4. What formal and informal mechanisms reinforce these procedures?
5. What is the degree of impact on the work itself, on staff, and on the initiative?

TABLE 2

Assessing Modifications to Unofficial Norms

Unofficial Procedures and Norms	Initiative Requirements	How the Workforce Interprets/ Perceives Changes to Norms	Possible Modification	Possible Repercussion of Modification

WHO? IN WHAT MANNER?

The assessment of current unofficial procedures and norms should begin with the individuals on the implementation team responsible for organizational change. These individuals should be excellent observers and listeners and have superior analytical skills. They also need to be knowledgeable and comfortable with change management and interviewing techniques. Their role is to evaluate the behaviors of the workforce and translate them into norms or procedures for a given workgroup or business unit. They need to examine and verify the patterns, determine how they are intertwined with the new behaviors, and if need be modify them to support the initiative.

READING 41–1

By evaluating the unofficial norms, an oil company learned that informal procedures encouraged hidden agendas, territorialism, individualism, and minimal career progression. After one year of initiative implementation, management had not changed the organization's norms and procedures, which created conflict for the workforce and ineffective initiative results.

42 Not Considering the Coordination Costs

	Preimplementation	During Implementation
Troubleshooting		✓
Preventative Action		

Self-Assessment Questions

1. Do you regularly look for hard measures so that metrics can be used to support cost estimations?
2. Do you know what your initiatives cost your organization in relationship to the benefits derived?
3. Do you track dollars (real or funny money) spent internally to support an initiative?

If You Answered No, Beware! The organization has no way to determine if the benefits gained from the initiative will outweigh the actual implementation costs.

WHAT NEEDS TO BE DONE?

Those responsible for driving the initiative must be very clear about expected returns, projected costs, and potential lost opportunity costs. Human coordination costs encompass the allocation of resources, time, and money. These elements impact the cost of implementation and must be properly budgeted.

Successful implementation requires more than having the right resources positioned in the organization; it also requires setting up the framework for resource allocation and accounting to ensure that the initiative is able to operate efficiently.

WHY? WHAT ARE THE BENEFITS?

Properly accounting for the coordination costs is key to an initiative's effectiveness. Often these costs are not controlled or even considered. Most organizations manage the direct costs to purchase equipment and materials and plan for start-up costs including hiring and training staff. However, indirect allocations and expenses are often missed. The costs of coordinating the effort after it is in place frequently are ignored because they can be difficult to identify and quantify. If unchecked, these indirect, less visible costs can surpass the gains that will be realized by the initiative itself.

HOW? A RECIPE FOR ACTION

The elements that comprise the organization's coordination costs for the initiative must be determined by using problem-solving tools. A generic checklist of typical functions and tasks that impact the dollars spent to support the human asset associated with any endeavor is shown in Table 1.

After you have identified these items, assess how they apply to your organization using the formula in Table 2 as a guide for estimating actual dollars. Consider each element in terms of its impact on the initiative and on cost containment and management. (In direct chargeback environments, organizations have already begun to think in terms of identifying all associated costs, and thus this identification process may have already been completed.)

TABLE 1

Typical Internal Coordination Functions and Tasks

• Team member salary. • Changes in compensation. • Job aids. • Communication dissemination. • Severance pay. • Change management plans. • Outplacement. • Recognition.	• Material. • Technology. • Lost productivity. • Site visits. • Organizational assessment—pre and post. • Team training. • Overtime. • Temporary staff. • Unlearning unwritten rules.	• Consultant fees. • Documentation associated with the initiative. • Training—on prerequisite and requisite skills. • Job retooling. • Facilities. • Data collection.

TABLE 2

Coordination Cost Formula

Formula								
Coordination Function or Task	Number of People/ Work Units Involved in the Task	X	Total Amount of Time Spent/ Materials Needed for the Task	X	Averaged or Detailed Cost per Hour for the Associated People	=	Dollar· Cost	

Even if the numbers obtained by the formula are "best guess" estimates, cost patterns among the various coordination elements will surface. The estimates will provide information about patterns and help the initiative owners begin to gather analytic data to substantiate the estimated costs. If the dollars appear to be very high, the initiative owners need to reassess the value of the initiative itself. Today cost/benefit and risk management issues are important, and an initiative should only be undertaken when the benefits outweigh the total costs.

WHO? IN WHAT MANNER?

Interpreting coordination costs is generally the responsibility of those who are evaluating the *go/no go* of the initiative. These individuals may not be involved with the number-crunching but they need to establish the importance of deriving such measures. They are responsible for ensuring that there is a staff in place capable of accurately identifying the coordination elements and assigning costs.

Not Making Use of Hard Data

	Preimplementation	During Implementation
Troubleshooting		✓
Preventative Action		

Self-Assessment Questions

1. Does the organization have public repositories of data that individuals involved in initiatives can access?
2. Does the organization have skilled data collectors and analysts?
3. Do individuals in the organization tend to rely upon analytic data when making decisions?
4. Are people in the organization conscious of the value of sharing the data they have at their disposal? Do they openly encourage others to access the data that they have?

If You Answered No, Beware! No way to validate decisions—reduces accountability and replicability.

WHAT NEEDS TO BE DONE?

Data analysis is very powerful. It provides a structure and methodology to gain meaningful and useful information. An organization cannot effectively implement an initiative without gathering and analyzing quantifiable and qualifiable data and acting upon it. Accurate, timely data are required by the initiative team to effectively develop the initiative's strategy, implementation plan, and evaluation methods. Data should be the primary source of information on timing, resource requirements, economic conditions, and customer needs.

Data collection methods must be accurate, appropriate, and have a clear purpose and disposition. This ensures that:

- Individuals collecting the information get facts that are necessary and usable.
- The risk of making decisions with the wrong data is minimized.
- Data collection is consistent and reduces the chances of random errors.
- The means for determining the reliability and validity of collected data.

WHY? WHAT ARE THE BENEFITS?

Several problems emerge when data are not used to make decisions:

- People rely on "gut feel."
- Personal and past experiences give a false sense of security.
- Individuals grow overconfident and behave as if they have solutions when they don't.
- Presumptions are made with limited facts.

Data highlight key characteristics and essential drivers of the endeavor. Without analytic data it is difficult to reach valid conclusions. Decision making becomes subjective or only reflects a small part of the picture over which the organization has immediate control or knowledge. Data verify information and clarify understanding of details and perceptions that impact initiative implementation.

HOW? A RECIPE FOR ACTION

The precursor to valid and reliable analysis is precise data collection. To ensure that appropriate and accurate data are collected:

- Clearly and explicitly describe the type of information that needs to be obtained. Do this by asking the right questions.
- Identify existing data—determine what sources of data are accessible in existing reports, documents, systems, and so on.
- Determine other sources for data collection. Do you need to gather the data using testing and/or sampling methods?
- Decide if there is a match between data received and the data definition previously established by initiative designers. Scrutinize the data to determine its reliability, validity, and usability.

> In an initiative to develop a customer-driven organization, the telephone customer service center does more than just report the time it takes representatives to complete a call. It also determines the percentage of time it takes a representative to paraphrase customers' requests during a call. Capturing customer satisfaction data has resulted in a more reliable predictor of customer requests being understood and solved.

Data collectors need to identify and retrieve hard-to-get information. They need to work around organizational confines and roadblocks and discern which individuals are willing to share information. The organization must recognize and be prepared to deal with individuals who are threatened by analytic data and avoid it. These people tend to discount its value and thus often fail to collect it.

Getting an organization to rely upon data will require:

1. Educate the workforce about the importance of data to an initiative's success. Focus on individual as well as organizational benefits.
2. Develop shared databases that cross organizational boundaries

and increase the information people can access. This requires inter-operability of platforms and systems.

3. Hold the implementation team accountable for gathering and researching data and using the information as part of the initiative design and implementation processes.

4. Hold the workforce responsible for accessing data as part of their daily operations. Encourage past data suppliers to demonstrate how the required data can be retrieved.

WHO? IN WHAT MANNER?

People who are responsible for collecting data need to openly distribute it. It is important that the data analysts network with each other. In some organizations the auditing and financial reporting staff are key data collectors and need to be involved in the data-collection process associated with any initiative. Whenever a new endeavor is started, a person from the initiative's team needs to take ownership for the data analysis process. This individual will:

- Determine who in the organization might have data from past initiatives or who might know about current performance.

- Ensure that data are ferreted out.

- Accept accountability for the team's obtaining, reviewing, and acting upon correct and accurate data.

Each initiative team member must have knowledge of data collection and analysis techniques. If no one is highly skilled, it is important that the organization provide training or seek consultative resources. This increases the probability that accurate data are used to make decisions about the current initiative.

READING 43–1

A hotel holds a weekly senior managers' meeting to review data and weekly progress. The statistics are communicated to all employees so that everyone within the organization can determine what should be done to improve last week's performance.

Compensation and Reward Are Not Aligned with the Initiative

	Preimplementation	During Implementation
Troubleshooting		
Preventative Action		✓

Self-Assessment Questions

1. Do compensation and reward systems reinforce structure and behaviors that support the initiative?
2. Is the compensation system well-received within the organization as an equitable method of rewarding value-added contributions?
3. Does the reward system inspire employees to increase their performance levels?

If You Answered No, Beware! No reward for the "new" performance results in people staying with the status quo.

WHAT NEEDS TO BE DONE?

Many companies are beginning to recognize the importance of aligning compensation and reward systems (i.e., financial incentives—all those mechanisms that are subject to taxation) to reinforce the initiative's objective. The compensation and reward systems should have a long-range focus that supports the strategies of the firm. The systems should be equitable and agreeable to both the organization and the workforce. They should challenge the performance and motivate employees to improve performance to support the initiative.

The senior management team, with the help of compensation experts, needs to sanction performance measures supporting the initiative such as financial indicators, employee productivity, process results and improvements, customer satisfaction, and retention indices. These measures should reinforce the goals of the organization and encourage the workforce to learn more about business operations. With the right mix of measures, performance can be equitably rewarded.

In today's flatter organization, compensation and reward systems can be key reinforcers to motivate employees to cross existing informal and hierarchical boundaries. It is important to establish internal control and monitoring mechanisms to prevent the system from becoming obsolete, out of sync with current initiative performance expectations, or counterproductive.

WHY? WHAT ARE THE BENEFITS?

Reward systems are strategic mechanisms to help achieve the initiative's goals. Used properly, they motivate the workforce to:

- Assume and accept the initiative behaviors.
- Contribute to the company's achievements and share in its prosperity.
- Increase knowledge, obtain the newly required skills, and improve performance.

When incompatible with initiative goals, the old, traditional reward system causes dysfunctional performance and encourages resistance to change. These inherited systems eliminate the incentive to adopt the new patterns and thwart creative thinking.

When dollars and talk do not agree, employees listen to the dollars and ignore management's voicing their desire for the adoption of new behaviors.

HOW? A RECIPE FOR ACTION

To develop a compensation and reward system, the organization should begin by evaluating the various systems that already exist. Over the last few years, the amount of public data on different compensation systems and their impact has mushroomed. Companies should evaluate the pro's and con's of various systems in light of their own philosophies, structure, measurements, prerequisites for workforce participation, management involvement, and results attained from installation. The financial impact on the initiative of implementing a new compensation system also needs to be evaluated in terms of short- and long-term opportunity costs, not just immediate dollar cost.

Variations in organizational culture and initiative expectations determine how well a compensation and reward system will perform. Table 1 provides variables by which to assess available compensation systems to determine their organizational appropriateness.

Once the comparison has been completed, the organization can focus internally and determine which system will link best to the initiative and produce the greatest results. Begin by computing the expected payback for the dollars invested in the reward and compensation system. The organization should determine the break-even point to establish minimum standards for a new system.

A critical variable of the compensation and reward formula is the effect of the measures on employee behavior. They should "stretch" performance. If standards are set too high, they may encourage employees to "flush work down the toilet" so they appear to be meeting their targets.

WHO? IN WHAT MANNER?

Often senior management sanctions a team to reevaluate compensation and reward systems and make recommendations for updating current programs. The team should include managers and

TABLE 1

Compensation and Reward System Evaluation Variables

Philosophy	▪ What is the theory and rationale for this system? ▪ What is the objective of this approach? ▪ What problem or purpose is the system trying to resolve? ▪ Is the philosophy aligned to your initiative? To your organization?
Measurement	▪ How is performance measured? ▪ What is the threshold performance level before bonuses/ rewards are paid? ▪ Have control points been established to monitor the process? ▪ What methods are used to evaluate effectiveness?
Structure	▪ Is it a formal or informal system? ▪ Is it a team based, individual focus, or combination system? ▪ Is there flexibility within the system? ▪ How does it need to be maintained? ▪ How are improvements suggested? ▪ Does system align with initiative?
Participation	▪ What are the roles of employees? ▪ How do employees participate in this system? ▪ Do managers directly contribute to the design of the system? ▪ Are managers used as coaches, facilitators, and/or mentors?
Obstacles	▪ What are the obstacles to this system in the current organization? In the future organization? ▪ What are the effects on management style? ▪ What are the impacts on the initiative?
Payoff	▪ Are bonuses and rewards given on an annual, quarterly, monthly, or weekly basis? ▪ What formula is used to calculate compensation and rewards?
Value Added	▪ Will the organization achieve the same or better results after the system is implemented? ▪ What kinds of payback do you expect to gain from initiating this system? Is this realistic? ▪ Will it increase productivity? ▪ Will it contribute to corporate value?

nonmanagers from various business units and compensation specialists to ensure a broad perspective. They need to benchmark information and suggest systems that will further a mix of organizational, work unit, and/or individual performance depending upon the initiative being supported. The team will need time and resources to conduct a comprehensive assessment. Developing accurate performance standards generally requires the help of compensation analysts and work-process analysts who can determine appropriate performance levels.

The leader chosen by senior managers to be held accountable for producing the recommendations must have the organizational and project management skills to direct the team. He or she must:

- Be respected, competent, and able to influence workforce acceptance of the new compensation system.
- Meet with senior management to provide updates and secure their continued support.

READING 44–1

A financial service company ties senior management compensation to initiative attainment. Forty percent of their incentive bonus depends upon how well initiative objectives are met.

Lack of Recognition for Small Achievements

	Preimplementation	During Implementation
Troubleshooting		
Preventative Action		✓

Self-Assessment Questions

1. Does the organization acknowledge people for minor, intermediate initiative accomplishments?
2. Does the organization thank individuals and teams for their extra efforts?
3. Are systems in place that individuals can tap into for nonfinancial recognition?

If You Answered No, Beware! Employees lack a vehicle to recognize others for initiative achievements, which results in lower morale, enthusiasm, and motivation.

WHAT NEEDS TO BE DONE?

As stated before, initiatives demand new behaviors that the current organization does not require. Employees behave in ways they "think" are expected and required of them. Focused recognition reinforces the demonstrated behaviors that the giver appreciates and helps the receiver to understand what is expected.

This type of reinforcement must be offered immediately, be easy to obtain, and given freely and honestly. It provides the incentives to entice employees to adopt these changes.

> Participatory recognition refers to nonfinancial acknowledgment of performance. It ranges from a simple thank you to nonmonetary tokens that employees give each other with no or minimal management involvement.

Employee-participatory recognition systems are needed to reinforce these new behaviors. Recognition is most powerful when it is tied to the accomplishment of initiative activities and publicized throughout the organization. There must be at least one company recognition system that encourages employees to celebrate the small achievements of the initiative. This allows people to boast about their accomplishments and fosters a motivated work force who continue to support the initiative's goals.

Some points for the recognition designers to remember:

- Adopted recognition options must avoid creating a "win-lose" situation—some get acknowledged, others don't. This condition demotivates employees.
- Recognition does not have to be monetary. A nonfinancial reward can have the same or greater value and incite the same rate of increased performance as a monetary reward. This is especially true of peer-based systems.

WHY? WHAT ARE THE BENEFITS?

Human beings need to be valued by others. Recognition connotes people's worthiness to the organization. All things being equal, it motivates the workforce to take on new challenges. It reinforces

acceptable behavior and minimizes variations. The degree of reinforcement generated by the recognition system will influence
future performance.

Recognition is a bridge between employee behavior and initiative expectations. Organizations need to create mechanisms to
encourage employees to match behaviors to the initiative's model.
When recognition systems are effectively designed, emphasize
positive initiative performance, and provide for continuous reinforcement at or above a perceived "reasonable level," they have
positive influence on behavior. Not meeting the minimum recogni-
tion/reinforcement expectations can lead to bitterness towards the
initiative and minimize involvement.

HOW? A RECIPE FOR ACTION

The organization needs to identify the behaviors that are to be reinforced. In essence, a recognition strategy needs to be developed to
support the initiative and organizational goals. Points that will
need to be assessed as part of the recognition planning process
include the items shown in Table 1. In some organizations a recognition committee is established to ensure that recognition is incorporated into the initiative plans.

Evaluate the appropriateness of each element for your organization and develop action plans to address them.

> **A NOTE OF CAUTION:** Take care to ensure that nonfinancial
> rewards aren't equated with unimportant rewards. Separate sys-
> tems may imply "unequal" value. This may have negative conse-
> quences, depending on how workgroups view the differences.

WHO? IN WHAT MANNER?

Managers, initiative leaders, and sponsors should be responsible
for taking a leading role in recognizing and celebrating initiative
successes. The recognition team needs to establish, implement, and
nurture the recognition system and regularly evaluate it. A recognition committee can assume responsibility to see that the system
is properly used. The goal for a nonfinancial recognition system is
that everyone be actively involved. This includes:

TABLE 1

Elements to Consider in the Recognition Planning Process

Elements to Consider

1. Employee profile—what kind of recognition will work with the various populations within the organization?

2. Preferences of senior management—must the systems be serious or is playfulness permitted?

3. Program structure—is the recognition system to be established permissible as a *separate* system, the *only* system, or an *additional* system?

4. Employee involvement—are employees allowed to participate at all levels of the recognition system, i.e., design, giving/receiving processes, and evaluation?

5. Performance factors—what specific goals or accomplishments should be recognized; for example, performance, productivity, behaviors, or activity completion?

6. Timing—is the system sensitive to insuring that recognition occurs immediately after performance has been achieved?

7. Continuous evaluation—is the system regularly measured to ensure that the nonfinancial rewards are being used and being frequently revisited?

8. Globalization versus localization—is the commonality of the system evaluated against site-by-site needs?

- Monitoring the number of people involved in giving and receiving recognition.
- The effectiveness of the recognition options/tokens used.
- The frequency of participation.

READING 45–1

A medical manufacturer enhanced its current recognition system by encouraging employees to acknowledge the contributions of co-workers. The human resources manager realized the importance of getting employees involved in designing the process. A team was established to determine what the peer system should look like, how it should operate, how to roll it out to the entire organization, and what techniques should be considered to maintain active participation of employees over time.

Ineffective Evaluation Methods

BARRIER 46

	Preimplementation	During Implementation
Troubleshooting		✓
Preventative Action		

Self-Assessment Questions

1. Does the organization analyze the process being used to launch its initiatives?
2. Does the organization report regularly on progress towards initiative goals? Are all affected groups receiving the reports?
3. Does the organization identify barriers to initiative progress and develop corrective actions?
4. Does the organization change tactics based on what it learns?

If You Answered No, Beware! Inability to monitor initiative progress and adjust plans.

WHAT NEEDS TO BE DONE?

The purpose of evaluation is to verify that the initiative conforms to a predetermined direction. The evaluation methodology should:

- Determine what the organization needs to know about the initiative.
- Establish a methodology for gathering the data.
- Analyze data.
- Develop action plans.
- Provide for feedback and and follow-up.

The evaluation process is a systematic, objective, impersonal, cross-functional review that reports on actual progress against goals and activities of the plan. Progress should be reviewed from top down and bottom up. Links need to be established from the work unit to the corporate objectives to reveal obstacles that might prevent achievement of the plan. Opportunities for improvement and variances need to be addressed and corrective action taken.

WHY? WHAT ARE THE BENEFITS?

Companies need to evaluate the *methods* used to execute the initiative as well the *activities* and *targets* related to the initiative's plan. Evaluation highlights alignment between goals and outcomes of the plan and facilitates the monitoring of progress on a regular basis. Some of the critical benefits of the evaluation process include:

- Providing the firm with information to determine if initiative performance matches senior management expectations.
- Assessing the impact on the initiative strategy.
- Identifying hurdles towards progress that trigger a chain of corrective responses.
- Examining progress objectively and keeping the organization focused on the goals.
- Highlighting achievements and barriers to accomplishing the plan's results.

Effective evaluation results in a consistent continuance of the initiative.

HOW? A RECIPE FOR ACTION

The design of an evaluation system should address several variables:

- Degree of accomplishment of each objective.
- Degree of consistency—how well the items in the plan relate to one another.
- Degree to which objective completion led to meaningful business results.

The high-level steps for an evaluation design are listed in Table 1. The evaluation should be preceded by a statement from senior management reconfirming the value of the endeavor, its purpose, and the expectations and standards at each step. The statement should tie measuring the effectiveness of individual workgroups' ability to achieve the initiative's critical success factors and objectives to the business strategy as a whole.

Outcomes of the evaluation should be documented and shared. An organization might consider developing an evaluation template that would provide a common framework so that comparisons can be made consistently throughout the organization and the lifecycle of the initiative.

TABLE 1

High-Level Evaluation Design Process

Step 1	Senior management establishes the importance of evaluation and gives support to the effort.
Step 2	Identify and define characteristics, standards, and requirements to be evaluated. Determine which should be assessed.
Step 3	Translate standards and requirements into activities that can be measured at stages of implementation or at workgroup levels.
Step 4	Gather and analyze data.
Step 5	Identify initiative progress in measured areas.
Step 6	Create action plans to address key evaluation results.
Step 7	Implement plans.
Step 8	Ensure that lessons learned are shared throughout the organization.
Step 9	Loop back to Step 1; relaunch the evaluation process.

The timing of the initiative's evaluation should be:

- Integrated into other organizational evaluation processes when possible—all are part of *one evaluation* because the organization is *one.*
- Conducted frequently throughout the process to provide useful feedback. (Weekly, monthly, or quarterly reviews are recommended so that changes can be made promptly. Intervals should be dictated by results of prior evaluations.)

WHO? IN WHAT MANNER?

The basis for evaluation—corporate standards and performance expectations for the initiative—should be established by senior managers. They should also participate in feedback sessions in order to monitor the outcomes of the endeavor. This involvement allows top managers to modify critical success factors, cancel aspects of the plan as required, and shift resource allocation.

Workgroup activities and results should be evaluated by the managers and employees who created them to ensure that:

- The evaluation is conducted.
- The workgroups are on schedule with plans.
- The issues are resolved and corrective action taken.

The workgroups should present their findings to at least two levels of management because managers at these different levels have different perspectives of corporate and initiative goals. This approach allows the reviews to "cascade-up" the organization and ensures that they are interwoven with the activities of the organization.

BARRIER

47 Not Recognizing Customer Needs

	Preimplementation	During Implementation
Troubleshooting	✔	
Preventative Action		

Self-Assessment Questions

1. Do you have a process for gathering customer feedback at all points of the initiative's lifecycle?
2. Have you trained your staff to understand the differences between wants and needs?
3. Can your staff work with the customers to establish true needs?
4. Can your staff think out of the box to develop products and services that provide customers novel business solutions?

If You Answered No, Beware! Your staff will engage in too many activities that don't create and execute high-value business solutions for customers.

WHAT NEEDS TO BE DONE?

For the initiative to have maximum impact, everyone must understand the difference between needs and wants and be able to effectively direct customers toward the former. The initiative sponsor must select or train the design team with this competency in mind.
   Initiative designers must understand that:

- *Needs* are *required* for existence.
- *Wants* are *desired* to make things better.

A problem that initiative designers and executors consistently face is not dealing with customers needs—stated and unstated—but instead addressing their wants. This manifests itself in two distinct ways:

- *Omnipotent omission*—not listening to the customers or involving them in the initiative process, either early enough or at all. This is a strategic planning and positioning issue that the organization must address by establishing standards for customer inclusion.
- *Disempowered reaction*—listening to the customer indiscriminately and trying to provide all-encompassing service that addresses *wants* more than *needs*. This is a training issue that requires educating employees on how to decipher customer input to establish true value-added requirements.

Whenever an initiative is undertaken, the customers' expectations must be considered a critical factor throughout the process, but with some conditions. Not all customers know what they need because they may lack the technical expertise to know what will provide value-added business solutions for the resources they spend. It is the job of the initiative expert to provide employees with enough information so they can help customers make wise decisions. If their initiatives are to add value, designers and executors must provide customers with usable information in language that cuts through "wants" and establishes needs.
   Consider for example an information systems unit that is undergoing re-engineering in order to provide better service to its customers. Customers are queried to establish what they need

from the area in terms of technology and applications support. If the information systems unit does not probe the customer correctly, it is presented with a *wish list* of "wants" that may not add sufficient value to justify the cost of instituting them. Unless those driving the initiative can structure the query and decipher the input, they use the information as "gospel" and set out to design a unit to accommodate customer *wants* that aren't needed nor that add value.

Another problem that confounds gathering clear need/want information is that the "experts" don't relate to the customers' business, nor do they listen to customer input about their problems. An ongoing dialogue between customers and customer contact employees must be established to create a loop by which customer feedback is provided, assimilated into the initiative, and reported back as recommendations for changes.

WHY? WHAT ARE THE BENEFITS?

A primary purpose for instituting any initiative is to increase returns to the organization—to provide a greater value-added process, product, or service. Part of the value-added equation includes customer input, because they receive the output of the initiative.

The design team must understand the initiative's technical nuances and how these relate to customer needs. They must also be able to discern those times when, even if the costs are high, it still pays to implement the initiative because of anticipated economic environmental changes—in other words, to spend money now to retain external customers. When these issues are addressed, the initiative will result in added value for the customer and more favorable cost ratios for the organization.

HOW? A RECIPE FOR ACTION

Begin the process by evaluating the skills of the design team in addressing:

- The technical issues and opportunities related to the initiative.

- The business issues, from a customer perspective, that are associated with the initiative.
- The differences between wants and needs and the distinctions between the business and financial perspectives.
- The business challenges faced by the customer looking for creative, alternative solutions to capture market share.

Team members must be proficient in each of these skills if they are to accurately assess input from customers, and the skills must be regularly applied in dealing with customers. The initiative sponsor can add or replace personnel if necessary to acquire these skills, or train/coach design team members to enhance skill levels for those who lack them. This must be done early in the initiative, before the team members begin customer contacts.

Part of the implementation process requires initiative team members to maintain an ongoing dialogue with customers to acknowledge and reflect progress in terms of meeting needs. This will require everyone involved with customers as part of the initiative plan to deal with the need/want dilemma.

WHO? IN WHAT MANNER?

The design team must demonstrate the ability to discern needs from wants. This skill cannot be taught by trainers (internal or external) who have no sense of the business or customers' operations. If senior people in the organization are skilled in this area, they are ideally situated to provide coaching for initiative team members. Otherwise, the organization can identify individuals who are skilled and recruit them as trainers/coaches.

Everyone who is a part of the initiative and who will deal with the customer must also possess investigative skills supported by problem solving skills that will allow them to:

- Assess customer issues to identify root causes.
- Develop value-added alternatives with/for the customer.
- Deal effectively with process issues that arise during the initiative's lifecycle.
- Raise business issues that result because of initiative implementation.

READING 47–1

A business services group wanted to improve the quality of its customer support. Customers were surveyed and included early in the design. The staff incorrectly assumed that whatever the customers said they wanted, needed to be done. They did not delve deeply enough into identifying actual customer needs. The organization ended up spending significant resources providing the customers unnecessary services. It couldn't understand why the customers weren't happy when every request was addressed.

Ineffectual Performance Appraisals

	Preimplementation	During Implementation
Troubleshooting		✓
Preventative Action		

Self-Assessment Questions

1. Is performance feedback collected from sources other than the manager?
2. Does performance feedback allow for two-way communication to discuss appraisal input?
3. Does the system include behavioral examples of performance to aid in corrective action?

If You Answered No, Beware! No change in behavior will occur unless individuals' initiative activities are measured and shared through a formal system.

WHAT NEEDS TO BE DONE?

The appraisal process provides a format to record individual and workgroup performance toward achieving the initiative's goals. It should be customized and modified to reflect the initiative activities being performed. Employees, manager, and workgroup should agree on the activities, with stated outcomes in measurable terms including standards, targets, and expected results. The goal is to provide maximum insight with minimal data.

When the employees or workgroup complete an activity, the manager should provide immediate feedback. The feedback, in the form of two-way communication, discusses accomplishments, obstacles to performance, and improvement suggestions. It should not only review what an individual or workgroup achieved but provide data on how and when people should change future initiative-related behavior.

> In customer-focused initiatives, the feedback might illustrate number and kind of delayed decisions, then explain how they potentially cost the company customers and how they might be eliminated.

WHY? WHAT ARE THE BENEFITS?

A cumbersome performance appraisal system makes it hard for employees to know what to focus on. Such an appraisal system makes it difficult to discern what actions should be taken to improve performance. These systems beg questions and use terminology open to interpretation by the individual.

> Be careful of systems that describe employee characteristics using words that are subjective and too generalized, such as dependability, punctuality, confident, and so on.

These systems also emphasize how well employees achieve numerical standards and don't reflect competency.

Including an evaluation of the achievements makes the appraisal less subjective and provides information on developmental/corrective actions that can lead to improvement. Effective evaluation is based on initiative-related behaviors and outcomes. It shifts focus from subjective opinions to the objective methods employees use to complete their work. The appraisal requires that evaluators record specific actions that provide actual examples of performance as well as suggestions for improvement.

HOW? A RECIPE FOR ACTION

The appraisal needs to review the performance of activities that complement the initiative. It needs to ensure that individuals accomplish specific, initiative-related objectives. One approach is to record the descriptions of activities, projects, and job behavior that support a given objective or well-defined work task. Attainment is reviewed against the pre-defined expectations for performance—these being set jointly by manager, employee, and workgroup. The evaluators can provide their feedback on a form such as the one modeled in Table 1.

TABLE 1

Feedback Form

Area of Performance/Competency:				
	What Specifically Will Be Done?*			
	Description of the Project	**Description of Responsibility or Task**	**Description of Associated Activities**	**Description of Observable, On-the-Job Behaviors**
Anticipated results				
Actual achievement				
Performance inhibitors				
Recommendation for improvement				
Plan for improvement				
Due date				

*May use one or more of the categories for any responsibility/task.

WHO? IN WHAT MANNER?

Employees, managers, and work teams (customers and peers, if appropriate) should provide feedback. The evaluators must accurately observe task-related behaviors and results to avoid conjecture; they must be sensitive to the recipient's perception of the feedback. No one should be included in the initiative appraisal process without training in the evaluation process. This includes manager, employees, and others.

Lack of Appropriate Training Methodologies

	Preimplementation	During Implementation
Troubleshooting		✓
Preventative Action		

Self-Assessment Questions

1. Is the training methodology based on adult learning theory?
2. Does the training support or reinforce the ever-changing environment?
3. Do training sessions ensure the practical application of material covered in class?
4. Does training allow for participants to experiment with new behavior and ideas?

If You Answered No, Beware! Training that doesn't specifically further the initiative results in wasted dollars and an inadequate workforce.

WHAT NEEDS TO BE DONE?

The training programs must be positioned to prepare participants for their new roles in rapidly changing business environments. Programs need to develop the leadership qualities that will make the initiative work. They need to reflect the new behaviors, interpersonal relationships, and thinking that are required in the new environment. Training should result in tangible behavior change and should improve the systems and processes of the company. The objective is to provide for comprehensive learning to aid initiative adoption. Programs tend to fall short of this objective because they do not show participants how to integrate the initiative into their work units or attain outcomes.

The training must provide a "big picture" understanding of organizational direction and clarify each person's role in the transition process. Today's workplace requires those in leadership positions to have a broad understanding of company drivers and operations. Training helps people to gain this knowledge and then to apply it in novel ways within their work units. Leaders need to learn to think about business situations in a different manner, so that multiple alternatives to any business problem can be generated and evaluated.

WHY? WHAT ARE THE BENEFITS?

Today's companies are more complicated and necessitate agility and flexibility to respond to the dynamic environment. Research shows that chaos moves organizations forward. Uncertainty forces companies to rethink and redesign the way they operate. To respond to these changes, training needs to adopt a new philosophy that accommodates changing business conditions.

Leadership training in many organizations is based on outdated methods that focus on creating the "ideal" company. This training theory envisioned a structured, core curriculum and was predicated on a "right" way of managing. It implied that if its principles were followed, the individual would be successful. This approach is no longer applicable and in fact is detrimental for managers in a competitive environment.

Training should be attuned to the way the organization "really" functions—how work gets accomplished and what it must do to be competitive. Training should develop skills in leaders that enable them to navigate the informal organization and deal with the fast-paced environment. Managers need to learn to influence informal systems and unofficial norms and procedures. These new requisites make it more difficult for trainers to keep their curriculum current, which raises questions about the effectiveness and high costs of these programs. This is especially true when highly changeable or low volume programs are developed by internal staff.

HOW? A RECIPE FOR ACTION

To implement a productive training program, designers must begin with a clear understanding of the general propositions of adult learning theory. Some points that will need to be considered as content is designed are shown in the checklist in Table 1.

Today's workplace requires that any training be done in a just-in-time mode. Developers need to focus equally on what needs to be included and on how it is to be presented. The practical application of information must be clear, so that participants can:

- Immediately apply what they learned in the session to their work environment.
- Understand the organizational strategy in depth.
- Explore various points of view and alternative solutions.
- Increase their responsiveness, flexibility, and agility.

WHO? IN WHAT MANNER?

Individuals who are knowledgeable about the business, the initiative, and adult learning process should be charged with establishing training programs to support the endeavor. Those who serve as content designers need to bring a fresh, global view of the environment and subject matter to the process. Depth of knowledge is important. If traditional trainers are included in the process, care must be taken that they don't focus on "old" curriculum methodology.

TABLE 1

Checklist to Assess the Workplace Focus of Training

General Propositions to Be Considered	How and What for Our Organization
1. What needs to be learned?	
2. What needs to be unlearned?	
3. What specific actions/skills can be immediately transferred to the workplace?	
4. How will the content accommodate adults' preference for learning by doing/experiencing?	
5. How will the program account for different learning styles?	
6. Where will learning best be done—in the classroom, through site visitations, or on-the-job?	
7. Is the learning work-related? Does it rely on work simulations, role playing, experimentation, and activities?	
8. Is the learning clearly tied to a practical business application?	
9. How will the new behaviors that are to be used on the job be supported? By whom?	
10. Is there a migration away from traditional curriculum to a focus on changing behavior, which necessitates learning how to: determine and influence unwritten rules and informal networks; establish standards, results, and requirements for activities; and determine customers' unmet needs?	
11. Is there creative, application-focused thinking on how to take data and apply them to new business situations?	
12. How does the program ensure that learners apply skills back on the job?	

READING 49-1

A retail chain requires as part of its initiative training that individuals must visit the company's locations and competitors' stores to learn about what their customers are experiencing and what new enhancements competitors now offer. They go on site visits with a list of questions that must be answered. They return to the classroom for group debriefing and to create group and individual action plans.

50 Allowing Inefficient Meetings

	Preimplementation	During Implementation
Troubleshooting		✓
Preventative Action		

Self-Assessment Questions

1. Does the organization have a standard model for how meetings are to be conducted—an agenda template and a process guide?
2. Would members of the organization rate meetings as a plus—something the organization does well?
3. Can your organization determine dollars spent on meetings—do you have a formula that is used to calculate meeting costs compared to benefits?

If You Answered No, Beware! The result will be costly meetings with no measurable impact, or that do nothing but reduce the enthusiasm of participants.

WHAT NEEDS TO BE DONE?

Meetings are at the heart of all initiatives. Depending upon the person, reporting level, organizational structure, and nature of the initiative; anywhere from 25 to 75 percent of the average day will be spent in group process. Ideally, the majority of the time will be spent on planning, problem resolution, and other initiative activities that require people coming together to provide input and make decisions.

It is the responsibility of initiative sponsors to appoint someone to assess and take action to improve the quality of meetings when necessary. This might involve introducing a meeting model and/or providing training to everyone involved in the initiative.

WHY? WHAT ARE THE BENEFITS?

Meetings are the typical vehicle most organizations use to accomplish initiatives. Many meetings are not as productive as they should be. They cost much and produce little. Nonproductive meetings need to be eliminated and inefficient meetings redesigned. Evaluate the return on dollars spent on meeting time. This ratio provides a prime, cost-control variable that organizations can use to improve the cost benefit ratio of any initiative.

> Meeting cost formula: Determining costs involves multiplying the number of people involved by an average per person hourly cost by the time spent in the meeting plus the ancillary costs (room, supplies, equipment, travel, other). This provides a total cost for meeting participation.

Often, people come together to do work that could have been done in some other way. Better use of alternative tools (memos, voice and electronic mail) will help to reduce the necessity for face-to-face sessions. This can reduce unnecessary costs and increase the productivity of initiative group sessions because the meeting focuses on key issues.

HOW? A RECIPE FOR ACTION

The organization must develop a companywide meeting management model. This ensures that everyone uses same set of meeting parameters and encourages *peer pressure* so that everyone follows the model. Some of the points that need to be addressed by the model are shown in Table 1.

The basics of meeting management need to be disseminated throughout the organization—generally in the form of a company handbook, pocketguide, or brochure, through e-mail, or on disk. This is best done through experiential workshops, which can be conducted with existing workgroups or made mandatory. The cascade (each successive organizational level to go through the workshop teaches the level below) or cadre (each individual trained to teach the workshop is expected to recruit and train another person) methods of teaching the model work best. Both methods develop many "trainers," so the training can be accomplished quickly with maximum buy-in.

> **A NOTE OF CAUTION:** Training lag time which hampers implementation—people don't apply the model because they're waiting for others to "understand" it, and inefficient timing results in minimal application.

WHO? IN WHAT MANNER?

The initiative sponsors must ensure that everyone involved in the initiative is familiar with the meeting management model adopted by the organization. Pre-initiative training on the model will guarantee that everyone in the organization practices good meeting skills. Key points:

- Make sure the organization has a meeting management model that *everyone* applies rigorously. (If none exists, the sponsors should take the leadership role and see that an appropriate one is instituted.)
- Develop a method for insuring that everyone's meeting skills (group dynamics) are at an appropriate level. If they aren't, planning will need to be undertaken to upgrade

TABLE 1

Meeting Model Guidelines

What	Why	How It Looks
Agenda building	Develops an understanding of the importance of the agenda as a tool for efficient/effective meetings. Clarifies the purpose of and gives direction to the meeting.	• No meeting is held without an agenda. • Everyone uses the same agenda format. • Meetings run according to agenda, including timing.
Meeting roles	There are certain roles that participants can assume to increase a meeting's productivity, such as note-taker, facilitator, timekeeper, process checker, or gatekeeper.	• Key meeting roles have been practiced, and everyone is able to assume roles upon demand. • Roles are accepted as a necessary part of each meeting.
Meeting ground rules	When the group operates under an agreed-to set of guidelines, meetings run more smoothly and more is accomplished. Each group needs to establish its own rules for behavior—these may be common to the organization or unique to each group.	• Posted/published ground rules are available for any team. • Everyone in the group abides by the rules it established—covered behaviors are not a source of conflict within the group. • New members are apprised of the guidelines and the modified group accepts or revises the rules. • Commitment is needed to keep the rules current: The group is willing to live by them. • Included in the rules are decisions on how to handle individuals or situations when rules are not followed.
Application of the cost formula	Everyone who participates in initiative meetings needs to become conscious of the associated costs.	• Each person evaluates the "value" of the meetings he or she attends and takes ownership to improve ineffective meetings. • A common costing formula is applied by everyone. • Meetings are regularly "costed out" to determine their value.
Evaluate effectiveness of agenda after each meeting.	At the end of each meeting, participants provide feedback about what they liked and what should have been done differently.	• Each person assesses effectiveness of meeting and offers improvement suggestions.

skills (the group may appoint this task to an outside vendor).

- Measure the effectiveness of the mode. Are people critiquing meetings they attend, checking to see if it is followed, and taking ownership to improve ineffective meetings?

READING 50-1

A high-tech firm realized that ineffective meetings robbed a great deal of each employee's time. To reduce meeting time and improve output, every person in the organization attended a meeting management workshop. This provided a model that everyone followed. Results: Fewer and better run meetings, increased attendance by critical players, accountabilities and action items assigned and delivered on.

BIBLIOGRAPHY

Birnbaum, W. S. *If Your Strategy is so Terrific, How Come it Doesn't Work?* New York: AMACOM, 1990.

de Bono, Edward. *Six Thinking Hats.* Boston: Little, Brown and Company, 1985.

Drucker, Peter. *Management: Task, Responsibility, Practices.* New York: Harper and Row, 1973.

Glanz, Barbara A. *The Creative Communicator: 399 Tools to Communicate Commitment without Boring People to Death.* Homewood, IL: Business One Irwin, 1993.

Gelatt, H. B. *Creative Decision Making.* Los Altos, CA: Crisp Publications, Inc., 1991.

Goodstein, Leonard D., Nolan, Timothy M., and Pfeiffer, J. William. *Applied Strategic Planning.* San Diego, CA: Pfeiffer & Company, 1992.

Gummesson, Evert. "Service Quality—A Holistic View," in Brown, S. W., et al. (eds.), *Service Quality: Multidisciplinary and Multinational Perspectives.* Lexington, MA: Lexington Books, 1991.

Hiam, Alexander. *Closing the Quality Gap: Lessons From America's Leading Companies.* Englewood Cliffs, NJ: Prentice Hall, 1992.

Juran, Joseph M. *Juran on Planning for Quality.* New York: Free Press, Collier Macmillan, 1988.

Katz, Amy. "Seven Guides for Facilitation," *Quality Digest,* December 1993.

King, Bob. *Hoshin Planning: The Developmental Approach.* Methuen, MA: Goal/ QPC, 1989.

Kirkpatrick, Donald L. *How to Manage Change Effectively.* San Francisco: Jossey-Bass Publishers, 1985.

Klubnik, Joan P. *Rewarding and Recognizing Employees.* Burr Ridge, IL: Irwin Professional Publishing, 1995.

Klubnik, Joan P., and Greenwood, Penny F. *The Team-Based Problem Solver.* Burr Ridge, IL: Irwin Professional Publishing, 1994.

Lawton, Robin L. *Creating a Customer-Centered Culture: Leadership in Quality, Innovation and Speed.* Milwaukee, WI: ASQC Quality Press, 1993.

McGregor, Douglas. *The Human Side of Enterprise.* New York: McGraw-Hill, 1985.

McLagan, Patricia, and Krembs, Peter. *On-the-Level.* St. Paul, MN: McLagan International, Inc., 1982.

Miller, Shawn. "Smooth Sailing for Your Quality Program," *Quality Progress,* October 1995, 101–103.

Myers, Isabel Briggs. *Gifts Differing.* Palo Alto, CA: Consulting Psychologists Press, Inc., 1980.

Nadler, D. A., Gerstein, M. S., and Shaw, R. B. *Organizational Architecture: Designs for Changing Organizations.* San Francisco: Jossey-Bass Publishers, 1992.

Ohmae, K. *The Mind of the Strategist.* New York: McGraw-Hill, 1992.

Peters, Tom. *Liberation Management—Necessary Disorganization for the Nanosecond Nineties.* New York: Alfred A. Knopf, 1992.

Rhinesmith, Stephen H. *A Manager's Guide to Globalization.* Homewood, IL: Business One Irwin, 1993.

Ross, Dr. Joel E. *Total Quality Management: Text, Cases and Readings.* Delray Beach, FL: St. Lucie Press, 1993.

Senge, Peter M. "The Leader's New Work: Building Learning Organizations," *Sloan Management Review,* Fall 1990, 7–23.

Schein, E. H. *Organizational Culture and Leadership.* San Francisco: Jossey-Bass Publishers, 1992.

Skutsky, J. J. "Conducting a Total Quality Communications Audit," *Public Relations Journal,* April 1992, pp. 32–48.

Webster's New Universal Unabridged Dictionary. New York: Barnes and Noble Books, 1992.

Wheatley, Margaret J. *Leadership and the New Science: Learning About Organizations From an Orderly Universe.* San Francisco: Berrett-Koehler Publishers, 1992.

Whitney, John O. *The Trust Factor: Liberating Profits and Restoring Corporation Vitality.* New York: McGraw-Hill, 1994.

INDEX